THE NEW WARS

THE NEW WARS

Herfried Münkler, 1951-

Translated by Patrick Camiller

polity

The right of Herfried Münkler to be identified as Author of this
Work has been asserted in accordance with the UK Copyright, Designs
and Patents Act 1988.

Originally published under the title *Die Neuen Kriege*,
copyright © 2002 by Rowohlt Verlag GmbH, Reinbek bei Hamburg

This edition © Polity Press 2005

The publication of this work was supported by a grant from the
Goethe-Institut.

Polity Press
65 Bridge Street
Cambridge CB2 1UR, UK

Polity Press
350 Main Street
Malden, MA 02148, USA

ISBN: 0-7456-3336-6
ISBN: 0-7456-3337-4 (paperback)

A catalogue record for this book is available from the British Library

Typeset in 10.5 on 12 pt Palatino
by TechBooks, India
Printed and bound in Great Britain by T J International Ltd, Padstow

For further information on Polity, visit our website: www.polity.co.uk

CONTENTS

ACKNOWLEDGEMENTS

The origins of my work on this book lie in a series of invitations to lecture on changes in war at the end of the twentieth century, on issues related to humanitarian military intervention and on the challenges posed by international terrorism. I have profited most of all from the questions, objections and assorted points raised in connection with these lectures.

In this way, I was constantly able to expand and clarify, to supplement and correct my initial reflections. Especially important for me were the invitations from the Vienna-based Institute for International Peace to a research conference in Reichenau an der Rax; the Clausewitz-Gesellschaft to its 2001 Congress in Berlin; the 4th Philosophicum in Lech (Arlberg), which was devoted to the issue of war; the annual meeting in Berne to report on the work of Swiss international law officers; the Bundeswehr Amt für Studien und Übungen in Waldbröl; the Theresianische Militärakademie in Wiener Neustadt; the Führungsakademie of the Bundeswehr in Hamburg; and the Katholisches Militärbischofamt in Berlin. The more politically oriented debates following talks at the Hans Seidel Foundation and the Heinrich Böll Foundation were equally invaluable, as were the discussions following lectures at the Stifterverband Baden-Württemberg in Stuttgart and the Carl Friedrich von Siemens Foundation in Munich. I would also like to mention the discussions with students and colleagues following lectures and talks at Bielefeld University, the Freie Universität, Berlin, the Johann Wolfgang Goethe University in Frankfurt, and the Ruprecht Karl University in Heidelberg. I have profited immensely from all these debates and discussions – some in a heated atmosphere, others in greater calm – and I owe a debt of thanks to all who extended the invitations and looked after my needs.

During the preparation of the manuscript, colleagues and associates from my Political Theory department and from the Berlin-Brandenburg Academy of Sciences read and commented on various drafts and raised further helpful questions and objections. I would like to mention by name Steffi Franke, Winfried Schröder, Skadi Krause, Dr Hans Grünberger, Dr Gerald Hubmann, Dr Klaus Schlichte and most especially Dr Karsten Fischer. Without their intellectual companionship, this book would not have existed in its present form. Admittedly, I have not always heeded the warnings and caveats offered to me in various marginal notes and letters, so that in this case I can state without reservation what is often merely said for the sake of it: that all the errors undoubtedly contained in the text are entirely my own responsibility.

As always in recent years, Karina Hoffmann copied out my handwritten notes, inserted additions, deleted unwanted passages and generally kept an eye on everything. Bernd Klöckener was the kind of editor of whom one always dreams but one rarely finds. His careful reading of the text, his proposals for a tightening of the language and his occasional encouragement to abandon sociological jargon were very helpful. Once again, however, the most important person for me was my wife, Dr Marina Münkler, with whom I repeatedly discussed anew the basic issues of the book, and who was an irreplaceable reader and intellectual companion during the final phase of my work. It is to her that this book is dedicated.

INTRODUCTION

In a process that long went unnoticed by the public, war has gradually changed its appearance over the past few decades. The classical model of war between states, which still largely marked the Cold War scenarios, appears to have been discontinued: states have given up their de facto monopoly of war, and what appears ever more frequently in their stead are para-state or even partly private actors (from local warlords and guerrilla groups through firms of mercenaries operating on a world scale to international terror networks) for whom war is a permanent field of activity. Not all but many of these are military entrepreneurs, who wage war on their own account and find various ways of obtaining the necessary funds. They sometimes receive financial backing from wealthy private individuals, states or émigré communities; they may sell drilling and prospecting rights on territory under their control, engage in drugs or human trafficking, or extort protection and ransom money; and, without exception, they profit from aid supplied by international agencies, since they control – or at least have access to – the refugee camps. But, wherever their resources come from, the financing of war is always an important element in the actual fighting – unlike in the classical conflicts between states. The change in modes of funding is a crucial reason why the new wars may stretch over decades, with no end in sight. Thus, if we are to understand the distinctive features of these new wars, we must always take into account their economic foundations.

Of course, although special attention will be paid here to the economics of war and force, this does not at all mean that ideological factors should be neglected. Ethnic-cultural tensions, and increasingly also religious convictions, play an important role in the new wars. Without ethnic and religious conflicts, the wars of the last decade in the Balkans, as well as those in the Caucasus and Afghanistan, would have developed differently or never have broken out in the first place. Such ideologies are a resource for the mobilization of support, and in recent times warring parties have fallen back on them to an increased extent. Clearly this is bound up with the fact that other sources of motivation and legitimation for the use of military force, which were prominent in earlier conflicts, have meanwhile been pushed to one side. This is especially true of social-revolutionary ideologies, which would have much greater significance if – as we still repeatedly hear it said – poverty and destitution really were the main cause of these wars. No doubt the uneven distribution of wealth is also relevant in the new wars, but it is by no means the case that military conflicts are most common where the poverty is most abject. Indeed, it may be argued that desperate want becomes more likely the longer military entrepreneurs have settled in a region and exploited its resources; and that the ending of a war brings with it no hope of political stability and economic recovery. The specific economy of the new wars, together with their long duration, ensures that the exhausted and devastated regions in question will never get back on their feet without extensive outside aid.

In view of the obscurity of the reasons for conflict and the motives for violence, I prefer to use the poorly defined but open-ended concept of 'new wars' – although I am well aware that they are not so new and in many respects even involve a return of something thoroughly old. A comparison with earlier forms of warfare may help us to work out the *differentia specifica* of these wars. First of all, they need to be distinguished from the classical war between states that still often shapes contemporary images of war.[1] But there is also the question of whether they can in a sense be described as a return to a stage prior to Europe's early modern statization of war; a look at that earlier period is a suitable way of bringing out similarities with the conditions in which the state is *no longer* what it was then *not yet*: the monopolist of war.

The constellations of the Thirty Years' War, in particular, exhibit many parallels with the new wars. It involved a characteristic mixture of private enrichment and hunger for personal power (Wallenstein, Ernst zu Mansfeld, Christian von Braunschweig), political drives for expansion into neighbouring states (Richelieu, Gábor Bethlen), intervention to save and protect certain values (Gustavus Adolphus), as well as internal struggles for power, influence and domination (Frederick V of the Palatinate, Maximilian of Bavaria) in which religious-denominational connections played by no means the smallest role.

In most of the major wars of our time – leaving aside the few instances of classical inter-state conflict between China and Vietnam, Iraq and Iran or Ethiopia and Eritrea – we find similar combinations of values and interests, and of state, para-state and private actors. The main feature is a multiplicity of interest groups which expect to derive more disadvantages than advantages from a lasting renunciation of violence, and which therefore find nothing to suit them in peace. The wars in sub-Saharan Africa (from southern Sudan through the Great Lakes region and the Congo over to Angola), the wars associated with the collapse of Yugoslavia, the armed conflicts throughout the Caucasus (most notably in Chechnya), the wars in Afghanistan since the early 1980s: all these bear much greater resemblances to the Thirty Years' War than to the inter-state wars of the eighteenth to twentieth centuries.

This kind of historical comparison may help to bring out the specificities of the new wars. We should examine three developments here. First, there is the already mentioned *de-statization* or privatization of military force, which has become possible because the direct pursuit of war is less expensive than in the past; light weapons can be obtained everywhere on favourable terms and no lengthy training is required in their use. This cheapening has to do with the second characteristic of new wars, the greater *asymmetry* of military force, so that the adversaries are as a rule not evenly matched. There are no longer war fronts, and, therefore, few actual engagements and no major battles; military forces do not lock horns and wear each other down, but spare each other and direct their violence mostly against civilians. One aspect of this asymmetry is that certain forms of violence that used to be tactically subordinate to a military strategy have acquired a strategic dimension of their own. This is true of guerrilla warfare, as it has developed since the end of the Second World War, and especially of terrorism. This brings us to the third characteristic tendency of the new wars: namely, a successive *autonomization* of forms of violence that used to be part of a single military system. As a result, regular armies have lost control over the course of war; to a considerable extent it is now in the hands of players for whom war as a contest between like and like is an alien concept.

In these conditions, does it make sense to retain an all-embracing concept of war to cover any deployment of force on a large scale?[2] With the end of the state monopoly, war has in fact visibly lost its well-defined contours: military force and organized crime go increasingly together, and it is often scarcely possible to distinguish between criminal organizations with political claims and the remnants of former armies, or armed followings of warlords, that keep themselves going through plunder and trade in illegal goods. 'War' has thus become a politically controversial concept. Is one promoting an escalation of violence if one applies the term to such phenomena? Or is one shutting one's eyes to new trends if one sticks to the traditional model of inter-state war and refuses to use the term for forms of violence below the level of the state? The political explosiveness of this question is especially evident in relation to recent forms of international terrorism.[3] Since 11 September 2001, what should and should not be described as war is no longer a question for academics alone, but an issue of possibly world-political importance. This book will seek to contribute to an answer.

I

WHAT IS NEW ABOUT THE NEW WARS?

The old empires and the new wars

Nearly all wars that have claimed our attention for a shorter or longer time over the past ten to twenty years have developed in the margins and breaches of the former empires that ruled and divided the world until the early part of the last century.[1] Thus, the Balkan wars linked to the break-up of Yugoslavia were most intense and lasted longest where the Austro-Hungarian and Ottoman empires collided with each other up to the early twentieth century, constantly shifting their spheres of influence in a succession of minor and major wars. Much the same is true of the armed conflicts and wars that have flared up in the Caucasus and elsewhere on the southern flank of the former Soviet Union, essentially in regions where the expanding Tsarist Empire and the shrinking Ottoman Empire contended with each other for supremacy from the eighteenth century onwards, and where it was only with great difficulty, and never on a permanent basis, that the Russians succeeded in bringing the mountain peoples under their sway. The eventual collapse of the Ottoman Empire at the end of the First World War led not only to the emergence of the Balkans and Caucasus as zones of war and conflict, but also to numerous confrontations in the Middle East, of which the Palestinian conflict has long been the most significant and dangerous.

As to Afghanistan, it retained into the twentieth century the role it had developed in the nineteenth as a buffer zone between the advancing Tsarist Empire and the British-ruled Indian subcontinent.

At the end of the 1970s the Soviet Union tried to exploit conflicts between Afghan modernizers and traditionalists, to expand its sphere of influence over the Hindu Kush and to acquire a strategic springboard between the energy-rich Far East and its potential Indian ally in the conflict with China.[2] The resulting war stretched over more than two decades and finally ended in the collapse of all state structures within Afghanistan. Whereas, in the 1980s, the United States appeared as the indirect adversary of the Soviet Union, by supplying the anti-Soviet Mujahedin with weapons and money, the Pakistani state took its place after the Russians withdrew and Washington lost much of its strategic interest in the region. Pakistan's military government hoped that the establishment of a friendly regime in Kabul would enable it to gain the strategic depth for a major war with India.[3] This interest derived in turn from a conflict that had grown out of the fragmentation of the Raj and the tensions and repeated hostilities between India and Pakistan. In the late 1940s, when the two states emerged as enemies from the bankrupt assets of the Raj, they were unable to agree on fixed frontiers between themselves – especially in the case of part-Indian, part-Pakistani (and part-Chinese) Kashmir, which remains a hotbed of tension and in whose inaccessible mountains a small war involving guerrillas and militias has been simmering for decades.

Finally, almost all the wars in South East Asia and Black Africa – from Indonesia through Somalia to Guinea or Sierra Leone – take place in regions which, until after the Second World War, were ruled by European colonial powers. Here, clashes between different states have been due not so much to frontiers inherited from the colonial period as to internal disputes over political influence and social-economic policy. Along with ethnic conflicts, which can be partly traced back to pre-colonial times and were used by the colonial powers to ensure their domination, religious and cultural differences not infrequently play quite a considerable role. Of course, in conflicts that often stretch over decades, these differences are so powerfully overlaid by power politics and economic rivalries that it is only rarely possible to decide what is a cause and what is a mere occasion. Moreover, warring parties are only too happy to exploit these differences as an ideological resource for the recruitment of followers and the mobilization of support. Even where people have lived smoothly side by side for decades in multicultural, multi-ethnic communities – as in Bosnia, for example – the outbreak of open violence turns ethnic and religious divisions into faultlines of a friend–enemy definition. In short, ethnic and religious oppositions are not usually the cause of a conflict, but merely reinforce it. It is hard to define the precise mixture of personal cravings for power, ideological convictions and ethnic-cultural oppositions that keep the new wars smouldering away, often for no recognizable goal or purpose. This skein of motives and causes makes it especially difficult to end these wars and to create a lasting peace.

Our first look at the geographical distribution and density of wars in the late twentieth and early twenty-first centuries shows that where a stable state came into being, as in Western Europe or North America, zones of lasting peace have developed, but that war has become endemic mainly in regions where a major empire held sway and then fell apart. It is true that, there too, new states immediately took their place in the world organization of the United Nations, but the great majority have proved to be weak and incapable of withstanding much pressure. These parts of the world have not seen the emergence of robust state forms similar to those of Europe. There can no longer be any doubt that the many processes of state formation in the Third World, or in the periphery of the First and the Second World, have been a failure.[4]

One of the main reasons for this failure is certainly the lack of incorruptible political elites who view the state apparatus as a source of tasks and duties rather than as a vehicle for personal enrichment. In many regions, the 'capture' of the state has served to increase the power or wealth of individuals, the two usually fitting together without difficulty. Contrary to a view widely heard in discussion of the causes of the new wars and the scope for ending them, poverty as such by no means points to a danger of escalating violence and war; the most that can be said is that the juxtaposition of desperate poverty and immeasurable riches is a significant indicator that conflicts within a society are likely to develop into open civil war. And the likelihood that such civil wars will not end after a short sharp outbreak of violence, but will grow into protracted transnational wars, increases with the suspicion that the disputed territory contains mineral resources whose sale on the world market would enrich those who are trying, if necessary through violence, to bring it under their control. Potential wealth is much more significant than chronic poverty as a cause of wars. A further factor may be revenue from affluent émigré communities, whose interests and loyalties may lead them to fund one or more of the warring parties and therefore increase their staying power.

In the emergence of new wars, none of the several causes may be singled out as the really decisive one, and so the various monocausal approaches (updated theories of imperialism or neocolonialism, explanations in terms of ethnic or religious contradictions) fall short of the mark. Yet the impenetrable web of motives and causes, which often leaves no prospect of lasting peace, is a direct consequence of the fact that it is not states but para-state players that confront one another in the new wars.

State-building or state-disintegrating wars?

Of course, the thesis that the new wars grow out of and end in the disintegration of states might be considered altogether too pessimistic, since, at least in a long-term perspective, it is possible that they are contributing to the formation of states – just as wars accompanied, sometimes interrupted, but ultimately carried forward the building of states in Europe.[5] The analogy cannot simply be dismissed, especially as the European state-building process that grew out of the disintegration of global powers was anything but linear and was never completed within one or two generations. But the decisive difference between the two is that the *state-building wars* in Europe or North America (the War of Independence and the Civil War certainly qualify as such) took place under almost clinical conditions, with no major influences 'from outside', whereas this has not been the case with the *state-disintegrating wars* in the Third World or the periphery of the First and Second Worlds. There, the wars leading to the collapse of young and still unstable states have been subject to constant political attempts from outside to influence the course of events, and above all have been linked into world market systems that make it impossible for them politically to control the development of their national economy. National wealth – in the form of oil and fuel ores, diamonds and precious metals – has not as a rule aided a self-supporting development of the economy, but has actually intensified conflicts over its appropriation and distribution. Thus, most of today's 'failed states' have failed not only because of the tribalism of societies with an inadequate degree of social and cultural integration, but also because economic globalization has had its most destructive effects precisely where it has not encountered robust states.

The exertion of outside influence, by both sides in the Cold War, certainly did not promote the consolidation of the states in question. Indeed, disaster was nearly always the result when the West or the former Eastern bloc, by sending military advisers or supplying weapons and equipment, tried to accelerate state building or to halt a process of erosion already under way. The Polish journalist Ryszard Kapuściński, an outstanding expert on Africa's political development over the past thirty years, has illustrated this point by referring to the Soviet-backed military regime of General Mengistu in Ethiopia:

> With Moscow's help, Mengistu had built up the most powerful army in sub-Saharan Africa. It numbered 400,000 soldiers; it had rockets and chemical weapons.... At the news that their commander had fled, this powerful force, armed to the teeth, collapsed in a matter of hours.... Mengistu's soldiers, having abandoned their tanks, rocket launchers, airplanes, armoured vehicles, and artillery pieces, set off, each man for himself, on foot, on mules, by bus, for their villages and homes. If by chance you find yourself driving through Ethiopia, you will notice in many villages and small towns strong, healthy young men sitting idly on the thresholds of their homes, or on the stools of humble roadside bars. They are the soldiers of General Mengistu's great army, which was to conquer Africa yet fell apart in the course of a single day in the summer of 1991.[6]

The suspicion that the new wars involve the disintegration rather than the formation of states is strengthened by the fact that, in the OECD (Organization for Economic Cooperation and Development) countries, the fiscal and integrative capacities of the state have passed their peak.[7] If, even here, the state administration has been unable to handle the task of steering complex processes at an acceptable cost – and since the mid-1970s the state's control and guarantee functions have been continually abrogated – it is scarcely surprising that comparable effects and challenges have regularly overwhelmed the much less robust and capable state apparatuses of the developing countries. Since most of their elites have not yet progressed beyond the stage of upholding patrimonial power and loyalty, their rule has usually descended into open corruption and the plundering of national resources. The need to keep their clientele happy with constant gifts and favours, combined with the potential to raise the necessary money by selling raw materials, issuing prospecting rights or trading in illegal goods, has rapidly led to a situation where ever larger parts of this income go to cover their own risk provision in the bank accounts of Western Europe or the United States. In many countries, painfully constructed elements of a functioning state and an elite ethos of public service were snuffed out in the briefest of intervals as state-building efforts were crushed between traditional tribalism and postmodern globalization. Unlike in early modern Europe, most

Third World countries had no opportunity to achieve development and the necessary degree of robustness.

This trend did not become truly dramatic, of course, until the inhibiting and destructive effect of tribalism and globalization on the state-building process reached such a degree that it promoted and helped to perpetuate war within the respective societies. In the agrarian subsistence economy that marked large parts of early modern Europe, wars would die down after a certain (considerable) time – once the country was ruined, the fields devastated and supplies consumed. But the picture is not the same in the new wars. They are linked in many ways to the world economy, through the phenomenon known as 'shadow globalization',[8] and are able to draw from it the resources necessary for their continuation. This is not the least reason why the American political and strategic theorist Edward Luttwak's idea of simply allowing the new wars to burn themselves out (in the hope that, after the exhaustion of the resources deployed in them, there would be a greater prospect of establishing a stable and lasting peace) so quickly turned out to be illusory.[9] The embargo policy pursued for a time by the West as well as the United Nations failed in almost every case to confirm the prognosis that increased consumption of resources in wars would put an end to them more swiftly;[10] for the warring parties usually managed to acquire the wherewithal, either by relying upon an ideological ally or a strategically interested regime, or by gaining access to the new forms of shadow globalization. This also explains why almost one in four of these wars has lasted longer than ten years.[11] In Angola the fighting has gone on for thirty years, in Sudan for at least twenty and in Somalia for more than fifteen. The war in Afghanistan, if it is now really over, will have lasted twenty-four years, while those in eastern Anatolia and Sri Lanka are approaching their twentieth year. Without support from outside powers, and especially without shadow globalization, this would scarcely have been possible. Shadow globalization, as the term is used here, includes the émigré communities that support either or both warring parties by means of money transfers, all manner of businesses, the recruitment of volunteers and the reception of wounded or exhausted fighters. The creation of refugee camps in neighbouring countries or under UN protection has played an important role in almost every one of the new wars. Refugee camps are by no means simply war's 'refuse dumps'; they are also its supply centres and reserve forces, where humanitarian aid from international organizations is at least partly converted into resources for the continuation of war.

Refugee camp in Kibumba, Zaire, 1994
Refugee camps have sprung up alongside all the new wars. International relief agencies address the human want and suffering, but the handouts of food and medicine also serve to keep the warring parties supplied. Photograph: Howard Davies/Corbis.

Short wars between states, long wars within societies

The long duration of the new wars scarcely differentiates them from the state-building wars of early modern Europe, which could also draw upon resources from external forces motivated by religious or ideological factors. In sharp contrast, the inter-state wars in Europe from the mid-seventeenth to the early twentieth century were, with a few exceptions, rather short; both sides sought to resolve their dispute through a battle that would pave the way for subsequent peace negotiations. Napoleon and the elder Moltke, in particular, brought to perfection this form of warfare based upon the concentration of forces in space and time. War was both declared and concluded in accordance with certain rules. It therefore had a precise definition in time, beginning with the declaration of war and ending with the peace settlement. Although the First and especially the Second World

War often broke these conventions, it is this model of inter-state conflict which still essentially shapes our idea of war: that is, a contest between soldiers fought in accordance with the codified laws of war. Only if some acts are not permitted in war can there be talk of war crimes that must be punished.

This has all changed in the new wars, whose course is determined by the dispersion, not the concentration, of forces in space and time, usually in accordance with the principles of guerrilla warfare. The distinction between front, rear and homeland breaks down, so that fighting is not restricted to a small sector but may flare up anywhere. A potentially decisive confrontation with the enemy is avoided at all costs, either because of a perceived unevenness of forces or because one's own troops are not suited to such warfare. The kind of combatant who dominates nearly all the new wars would have had no place in those that shaped the course of European history in the eighteenth to twentieth centuries. Typically, then, the new wars lack what characterized the inter-state wars: the decisive battle which, for Clausewitz, was the 'real centre of gravity of the War':

> The great battle takes place for the sake of itself, for the sake of the victory which it is to give, and which is sought for with the utmost effort. Here on this spot, in this very hour, to conquer the enemy is the purpose in which the plan of the War with all its threads converges, in which all distant hopes, all dim glimmerings of the future meet; fate steps in before us to give an answer to the bold question.[12]

Such questions are not posed in the new wars; there is no time or place where all the threads converge and a decisive result is sought.[13]

Nearly every party in the new wars follows the principles of what Mao Zedong called 'protracted warfare'. For Mao, however, the tactic of withdrawal and dispersion after lightning attacks was only a means to wear down a numerically and technologically superior enemy, to sap its strength in order eventually to achieve equilibrium, so that the initially weaker side might then gradually move on to the strategic offensive and seek a military resolution of the war.[14] Most players in the new wars, on the other hand, content themselves with what Mao called 'strategic defensive'; that is, they use military force essentially for self-preservation, without seriously looking for a military resolution to the war. If both sides conduct the war with this aim in mind, then clearly, with sufficient internal or external funding, it can theoretically last for ever. Often it is no longer even identifiable as war, since there is scarcely any fighting and the violence, as it were, seems to be dormant. But then it suddenly breaks out anew, and the war may acquire fresh intensity before dying down again and appearing to come to an end. The concept of 'low-intensity wars' is supposed to express just this concatenation.[15]

Different forms of warfare draw their strength and energy from differently organized economies. If the basis of classical inter-state wars was a centrally controlled economy with autarkic potential, supplemented at least since the French Revolution with total mobilization, the economy of the new wars is characterized by high unemployment, high levels of imports and a weak, fragmented and decentralized administration: 'It could be said the war economy represents a new type of dual economy, typical of peripheral regions exposed to globalization.'[16]

Whereas classical inter-state wars were separated from peace by legal acts such as a declaration of war and a peace agreement, and whereas they knew no intermediate status between war and peace (as Hugo Grotius pointed out in his great work *De iure belli ac pacis*[17]), the new wars have neither an identifiable beginning nor a clearly definable end. Only very rarely is it possible to set a date on the cessation of violence, or on its flaring up again. Classical wars ended with a legal act which assured people that they could adjust their social and economic behaviour to conditions of peace; most of the new wars, by contrast, come to an end when the overwhelming majority of people behave as if there were peace, and have the capacity over time to compel the minority to behave in that way too. The problem is, of course, that in such cases the defining power rests not with the majority but with a minority. Where there is no state executive powerful enough to impose the will of the majority, the ones who decide on war or peace are those most prepared to resort to violence. They hold the initiative and impose their will on everyone else. Thus, another reason for the protracted nature of internal and transnational wars is that, if even small groups are unhappy with the emerging peacetime conditions, it is an easy matter for them to rekindle the flames of war. Since, in intra-state wars, every group capable of violence must be won over to the renunciation of violence, peace *agreements* ending the war are replaced by peace *processes* in which the warring parties have to be sworn to mutual consumption of the peace dividend. As a rule, however, these peace processes are successful only if an outside arbiter is capable of suppressing the violent options (if necessary through superior force), and if sizeable funds are introduced to make the dividend sufficiently attractive. This being so, it is scarcely surprising that peace processes end more often in failure than in success.

Victim totals, refugee camps, epidemics

In the wars that were fought up to the early part of the twentieth century, roughly 90 per cent of those killed or wounded would have been defined as combatants under international law. In the new wars at the end of the twentieth century, the profile of victims has been almost the exact opposite: some 80 per cent of the killed and wounded were civilians and only 20 per cent were soldiers on active service.[18] One explanation for this turnaround should be sought in the decline in the number of inter-state wars and the dramatic rise in the number of intra-state and transnational wars. But that is not all there is to it. More critical is the fact that, in the new wars, force is mainly directed not against the enemy's armed force but against the civilian population, the aim being either to drive it from a certain area (through 'ethnic cleansing' and perhaps even the physical annihilation of whole sections of the population) or to force it to supply and support certain armed groups on a permanent basis. In the latter case, which is typical of the new wars, the boundaries between working life and the use of force become blurred. War becomes a way of life: its players make a living out of it, and not infrequently amass considerable fortunes. In any event, in the short term wars come to involve robbery and plunder, in the medium term forms of slave labour, and in the long term the development of shadow economies in which exchange and violence are inseparably bound up with each other.[19] Hence, the belligerents and groups associated with them have an increasing interest in the continuation of war,[20] and the means of forcibly asserting this interest is no longer the decisive battle but the massacre.[21] Unlike on the battlefield, where an armed opponent capable of putting up a fight is forced to submit to the political will of the other side, extreme violence is used here to intimidate an unarmed civilian population into doing whatever the armed group commands. The economy of robbery and plunder nearly always rests upon an extensive organization of fear. The new wars exhibit a distinctive management of fear, which the armed side constructs and organizes against the unarmed. This leads to a widespread breakdown of discipline among the armed group: soldiers become looters for whom the laws of war or any kind of military code of punishment no longer enter the picture; and a strong sexualization of violence produces phenomena ranging from almost daily orgies or veritable strategies of rape through to the ever more common mutilation of victims and the displaying of body parts as war trophies.[22] 'The war', Hans Christoph Buch reported from Liberia:

is turning things inside out. This metaphor becomes literally true when you look at the severed head that replaces traffic lights at a road junction in Monrovia, telling drivers not to proceed any further. Only on closer inspection do I realize that the rope strung across the street, which blocks access to the bridge, is in fact the intestines of the dead man, whose headless body sits as a macabre still life on an office chair.[23]

Especially characteristic of the new wars, however, is the association of military violence with starvation and epidemics. From the late seventeenth century onwards the statization of war, and the strategic orientation to its earliest possible resolution, broke up the premodern troika of famine, pestilence and war (also represented, for example, in the Horsemen of the Apocalypse[24]) and entailed that times of war were no longer necessarily accompanied by disastrous famines and epidemics.[25] By contrast, in most wars of the last twenty years, those who are unable to get food by force of arms are condemned to starve or to face death from disease amid the wretched hygiene conditions of the refugee camps – a tendency sometimes reinforced by the use of economic sanctions to bring belligerent regimes into line without actually applying force against them. Regularly it is young children, women and old people who pay the highest price, even if they are not direct victims of military violence. And since only part of this price – or none of it – is included in the final tally of the costs of war, the percentage of civilians among the casualties should probably be set higher than it is.

It is no accident, then, if the new wars are visible to us mainly through the refugee flows, slum camps and famished populations, but not in fighting between armies and decisive battles. The trickling of military violence to the outer reaches of the social capillary system has turned war into a phenomenon that is not only without beginning or end but also without any clear contours. The new wars know no distinction between combatants and non-combatants, nor are they fought for any definite goals or purposes; they involve no temporal or spatial limits on the use of violence. Intra-state wars have a strong tendency to jump across the boundaries of the region in which they originated and to turn into transnational wars in the briefest space of time. And, finally, the players in these wars enter into myriad links with international organized crime – whether to sell war booty, to dispose of illegal goods or to provide themselves with weapons and ammunition[26] – so that the question of whether certain forms of violence are acts of war or merely criminal acts can be posed in different ways. But what does 'crime' mean, when

there is no longer a state structure? The war in Colombia is probably
the most conspicuous example of this kind of diffuseness,[27] but the
Chechen war is also conducted by both sides in such a way that it
is no longer clear where the boundary lies between acts of war and
ordinary violent crime:[28]

> Not surprisingly, since the gun and the black market work hand in
> hand in war, these people tended to be not just ordinary criminals
> out for a fast buck but uniformed criminals, members of the most
> extreme and murderous Chetnik paramilitary groups. It was beyond
> irony that many of the same fighters who got drunk at the Hotel Bosna
> and then would career through the streets of Banja Luka, lobbing the
> occasional grenade through the front window of a Muslim home, were
> those the Muslims had to pay to get the things they needed in order to
> survive.[29]

To have separated the use of force from commercial activity, and to
have imposed that distinction as a trend in society, is one of the often
overlooked achievements of the state, brought about only because
it had a de facto monopoly on war. This suggests that the new wars
should be defined first of all in contrast to classical inter-state wars,
and that what is new and distinctive about them should be analysed
within that framework.

Privatization and commercialization: warlords, child soldiers, firms of mercenaries

The de-statization of war, which finds its plainest expression in the
growth of para-state and private players, is driven not least by the
spreading commercialization of military force.[30] One of the elements
in the new wars is the state's loss of its monopoly of military force.
When it features in them at all, it does so only together with private
firms which, partly for ideological reasons but mainly for robbery
and plunder, have joined the ranks of the belligerents. The much-
feared 'Chetniks', those paramilitary groups and gangs who fought
as volunteers on the Serbian side in the wars accompanying the disintegration of Yugoslavia, acted in many cases out of primarily economic motives: the booty from the houses of those they drove out
and murdered enabled them for a while to live a life about which they
could only dream as ordinary civilians. The new wars give contemporary relevance to the motto variously attributed to the Spanish

general Spinola, the mercenary leader Ernst zu Mansfeld and the Swedish king Gustavus Adolphus: that war must continually feed war. Paramilitary units, warlord troops, local militias and mercenary bands are not equipped and paid by functioning states that tax part of the social surplus, but usually have to find ways of supplying themselves. Increased use of violence against civilians is a direct result of this, but it is the only means that armed groups have of supporting themselves. Moreover, in civil wars it is the most effective means, since anyone under arms not only has better chances of survival, but can also live better and more securely when life's necessities are primarily distributed *manu militari*.

Local warlords and transregional entrepreneurs come forward as the main protagonists and profiteers in the de-statization of war.[31] Those, in particular, who control and are able to plunder large areas of a collapsed state claim for themselves the chief attributes of state power – not, of course, to push forward the arduous process of state building, but to garner the additional advantages that come from international recognition (economic support, access to international markets and the possibility of transferring their ill-gotten gains abroad to protect them from rival warlords). In the case of warlords, then, the claim to the attributes of state power does not involve tying themselves down or taking on new obligations out of which a state-building process might develop over time. It is merely a continuation of booty-hunting by other means.

Warlord configurations differ from civil war configurations in their 'use of violence as a means of regulating markets' and in 'the transformation of violence into a commodity or service'.[32] Hence, warlords are mostly found where markets receive no protection from the state and non-violent commodity-producing economies are combined with the violent acquisition of goods, services and legal titles – which is always the case when the structure of the state has definitively broken apart. But whereas, in the classical forms of the nineteenth and early twentieth centuries, warlordism rested upon the structures and conjunctures of an agrarian economy, it has since penetrated the subcultures of urban youth (its largest source of recruitment), where it uses the culture-industry settings of rap or reggae and corresponding promises of consumption and status to draw in and motivate future fighters. In some warlord configurations, sunglasses and kalashnikovs have become iconic signs of a readiness to engage in brutal unpredictable violence. In a number of such groups, however, violence is used simply to preserve their members' physical existence. Hartmut Diessenbacher has proposed the term 'overpopulation warrior' to describe such individuals, thereby making it clear that they threaten and use violence not to acquire luxury goods and status symbols but to ensure their bare survival.[33]

Often, of course, the two warlord types (classical rural and modern urban) cannot be precisely distinguished from each other, or the political and economic situations are such that there is a fluid transition between the two. In all cases, however, warlords quite deliberately use refugee camps both as recruiting grounds and as places to fall back on where they can help themselves to international relief aid. 'International relief for the poor, starving population is an inexhaustible source of profit to the warlords,' writes Ryszard Kapuściński. 'From each transport they take as many sacks of wheat and as many litres of oil as they need. For the law in force here is this: whoever has weapons eats first. The hungry may take only that which remains.'[34] International aid has thus frequently become part of the local war economy: what was supposed to relieve hunger and poverty becomes a resource of war.[35]

Along with the warlords, child soldiers have made their entry into the new wars. The UN estimates their total number around the world at approximately 300,000.[36] The fact that children, many of them under fourteen years, can be used at all in military hostilities is due not least to the technical development of firearms, whose average weight has continually fallen at the same time that firing frequency has increased. They have also been shrinking in size, so that many look as if they were specially designed for children rather than adults.[37] Children do not need a long period of training before they can be deployed as fighters, and their comparatively undemanding nature and low awareness of risks make them a cheap and effective instrument in the application of force. The Khmers Rouges in Cambodia used such soldiers no less than various groups in Afghanistan and the warlords in Black Africa. These adolescents, for their part, often consider a gun as the only means of getting food and clothing, or as the simplest way of acquiring desirable consumption goods and status symbols.

One major impetus behind the new wars is the combination of structural unemployment and the disproportionately high representation of young people in the total population who are largely excluded from the peace economy. They are not subject to the disciplining mechanisms of regular work, nor do they have access to the world of consumption. Peter Scholl-Latour, repeating the explanations given him by an African interlocutor, asks: 'So how can a child soldier of twelve or fourteen, who would otherwise vegetate as a street urchin or a casual labourer, do better than terrorize adults

Child soldier with automatic weapon in Burma, 2000
A gun increases the chances of survival in intra-state wars. Automatic weapons have made it possible to use children in war, and their relative lack of concern in the face of danger, together with a lust for adventure and the prospect of regular provisions, have drawn teenagers to war by the thousand. Photograph: Ullstein.

with his kalashnikov and demonstrate his omnipotence by shedding blood?[38] Such power fantasies, which these armed adolescents can act out without hindrance, play an important role along with the overcoming of hunger and destitution. As Hans Christoph Buch reports from the war in Sierra Leone:

> Although you risked your life crossing the road junction, the gang warriors ceased firing at the approach of the journalists and asked the fighters hidden among the wrecked cars on the other side to allow the strangers through. All parties in the civil war followed this rule – something I can explain only by the fascination that the media held for them. Stirred up by violent videos, the young people had no greater wish than to appear on television themselves, and they would strike up a Rambo posture in front of the TV crews. A human life in Monrovia was worth no more than five dollars, and for even less the armed teenagers ... were prepared to execute a hostage in front of a running camera.[39]

A final element in the fantasies of omnipotence is the free rein given to sexual needs. These gun-toting adolescents have been responsible for many particularly gruesome rapes and mutilations of sexual organs. Michael Ignatieff, who knows better than almost anyone else how to combine reportage with analysis, has pointed out that the increased cruelty and brutality of the new wars is essentially due to the increased involvement of these armed youngsters. 'In most traditional societies', he writes:

> honour is associated with restraint, and virility with discipline. . . . The particular savagery of war in the 1990s taps into another view of male identity – the wild sexuality of the adolescent male. Adolescents are supplying armies with a different kind of soldier – one for whom a weapon is not a thing to be respected or treated with ritual correctness but instead has an explicit phallic dimension. To traverse a checkpoint in Bosnia where adolescent boys in dark glasses and tight-fitting combat khakis wield AK–47s is to enter a zone of toxic testosterone. War has always had its sexual dimension – a soldier's uniform is no guarantee of good conduct – but when a war is conducted by adolescent irregulars, sexual savagery becomes one of its regular weapons.[40]

Ignatieff's account may also be expressed in figures. While international organizations estimate that 20,000 to 50,000 women were raped in the Balkan wars of the last ten years, Human Rights Watch set the corresponding figure during and after the genocide in Rwanda at more than a quarter of a million.[41] The violence used against civilians in the new wars is mainly violence against women.[42] Practices range from 'ethnic cleansing' strategies (which are associated with systematic rape) through destruction of the cohesion and moral norms of a society (rape especially stigmatizes young women and makes them alien bodies within the community) to extension of the demand for war booty to include forced sexual intercourse with women and girls in newly occupied territory. The descent into sexual barbarism of which Ignatieff speaks can be seen mainly where new wars shatter and ravage societies with a traditionally rigid sexual morality. Here the opportunities for sex at the point of a gun are especially tempting, and the social consequences especially devastating, since the social groups in question can no longer reproduce once a large part of their young women have undergone the stigma of rape.

In addition to the emergence and growth of warlordism and the deployment of cut-price child soldiers, the tendency to privatize and commercialize war is apparent not least in the wider involvement of mercenaries in nearly all these wars – from the West European adventurers and fortune hunters who on their own initiative joined one of the parties in the Balkan wars, usually for rather low remuneration, through to the highly professional London-based security businesses with branches around the world, such as the Control Risks Group, Defence Systems Ltd, Sandline International, Saladin Security, Gurkha Security Guards and, above all, Executive Outcomes, which can supply well-trained military personnel as well as aircraft and helicopters and elaborate security systems.[43] Among their clients are heads of state who can no longer rely on their own army and presidential guard to crush uprisings, as well as internationally active corporations that turn to mercenaries to protect their production sites in hotbeds of war and insurrection. In Africa there is a widely held view that a single Executive Outcomes mercenary is worth as much as a whole company of native soldiers.[44] The new war mercenaries also include the Mujahedin of Chechnya and Bosnia, Afghanistan and Algeria, who are paid out of the petrodollars of Arab states or private individuals to fight for the maintenance of religious bonds and cultural values. At least some of these mercenaries should be classed as belonging to fighting units more or less officially created and trained by Western states; most famously, this is the case of the French Foreign Legion, but it also applies to Gurkha units within the British army, to the South Lebanese Army that Israel maintained for a while to secure the buffer zone on its northern frontier and, not least, to the Afghan Northern Alliance, which for a few months was, as it were, taken into the service of the Anti-Terror Coalition.

From Mujahedin networks to contingents of hastily recruited fighters, from distinguished-looking security firms linked to the top addresses in the arms trade through to rowdy adventurers noted for their overindulgence in alcohol and for going weeks without washing to preserve the traces of battle: none of these consists of state subjects fighting out of a mixture of political duty and patriotic attachment to a cause, but rather of individuals driven mainly by financial gain, a lust for adventure and a range of ideological motives. There can be no doubt at all that this motley group – whose pay may only cover immediate necessities but may also reach the heights of $15,000 a month[45] – is removing more and more of the limits to the violence and brutality of war. The Hague Land Warfare Convention, together with the Geneva Convention and the prohibitions and restrictions contained in its additional protocols, are scarcely ever respected in the new wars. The main reason for this is that the countries that form the traditional target group of war-related and international law are of little significance for the course of the new wars. The so-called regular armies, which officially defend the state, are mostly nothing other than marauding bands, and the half-state, half-private players are not really subject to the sanctions threatened under international law, especially as few powers are willing to enforce the law, to arrest war criminals and, eventually, to organize costly court proceedings that may last for years. The passing notion that world politics was generally changing for the better, after the end of the East–West conflict and the decline in the number of inter-state wars, has thus turned out to be a great illusion.[46] The number of wars has increased over the longer term,[47] and the chances are diminishing that violence can be contained by legislation and the courts. While many intellectuals in Western Europe and North America reflected on global internal policy, global civil law and democratic peace,[48] war has torn down the protective fencing and established itself as an independent presence on the periphery of the zones of prosperity, a – quantitatively if not formally – new mode of income generation. War enables many people to make a living: it provides them with a means of generating considerable income in the short term and of living out blocked fantasies without restraint; it also endows a few with huge fortunes and indescribable wealth. It might be objected that things have always been so, that they were much the same in traditional inter-state wars. But the crucial difference is that what used to be a concomitant of war, more or less pronounced in each particular instance, has become the central focus and true goal of many new wars.

Civil wars, small wars, illegal wars: the quest for concepts

How should such wars be conceptualized? In much of the literature,[49] one finds a concept of civil war that has the not-to-be-underestimated advantage of linking up with long traditions of political thought and therefore offering analytic instruments for the theorization of new wars. These traditions stretch back to Sallust's book on the Catiline conspiracy in the late Roman Republic or to Thucydides' observations on the mutual killing of the democratic and aristocratic parties in Kerkyra. 'Civil war' is the classical complementary concept to 'inter-state war', and it may seem that several features of the new wars call for use of this term. Yet, precisely because it stands in a long tradition of political theory, the concept of civil war obscures what is specific: namely, their insertion into the process of economic globalization or shadow globalization, and the development of new constellations of interests geared not to the ending of war but to its theoretically endless continuation. In the classical civil wars, from antiquity to the modern age, the party that emerged victorious from a massive outbreak of violence wrested power within the state and tried to perpetuate in peacetime what it had achieved through war. Civil wars are intra-state conflicts over power and rule that are settled by violent means. Even if they drag on for several years, as did the Spanish Civil War, the different parties seek to capture state power in order to assert their political interests and ideas. This is not the point in the new wars: the existence of long-term warlord configurations does not fit well with the concept of civil war, although there can be no doubt that many of the new wars display elements of the classical civil war. But it is above all the political connotations of the concept of citizen [*Bürger*], central to the definition of civil war [*Bürgerkrieg*], which cannot be reconciled with most of the features of the new wars.

If the concept of civil war is stronger in the traditions of political theory, the concept of the small war (nowadays increasingly used as a variation on 'low-intensity war'[50]) has done greater service in writings on the history of war. It is not only since the anti-Napoleonic guerrilla war in Spain that the small war has been a constant accompaniment of the large war. In that war, Spanish raids and ambushes continually wore down the Armée d'Espagne, threatening supply lines and increasingly demoralizing the French forces, with the result that the numerically inferior British forces under Wellington were able to hold their own on the Iberian peninsula. But already in the eighteenth century small wars, with their use of light troops, chasseurs and hussars, had had the function of protecting the movements of the main army, preventing the advance of enemy troops, repeatedly cutting their supply lines for short periods and generally inflicting the maximum economic damage on the enemy by means of plunder and devastation.[51] Whereas large wars directly targeted the enemy's military forces in order to break his political will, small wars struck more and more at the enemy's economic base in order, indirectly, to weaken his ability to impose his political will by military means. Twentieth-century theorists who defined guerrilla warfare as the royal road to decolonization and revolution in the Third World had to abandon this classical combination of small and large war, but in so far as they relied on the development of regular or semi-regular troops out of the partisan ranks they too established a modified link between the two.[52] As Christopher Daase and others have pointed out, any such combination no longer applies in the new wars: small war changes from a supportive instrument for large war into its functional replacement. But such points have long been made chiefly with regard to the consequences for the international order, and not so much for the purposes of understanding the evolution of new wars as such. They therefore place more emphasis on the aspect of strategic asymmetry than on the privatization and commercialization of war.

Another attempt to conceptualize recent developments is Wolfgang Sofsky's use of the term 'wildcat wars' [*Wilde Kriege*] to reflect the re-emergence of marauding bands, the increasing frequency of massacres and the systematic use of rape as a war measure.[53] To be sure, this concept does bring out some of the characteristic features of the new wars, but it directs our attention away from the ideological resources of the belligerents and the economic aspects of these wars in which long-term, thoroughly purposive interests play a major role; a stress on confused rage and extreme bloodlust does not adequately grasp, or does not grasp at all, either the ideological or the economic aspect. In particular, the interweaving of infra-state players (warlords, mercenary firms, terror networks) with globalization processes is not sufficiently taken into account, either in Sofsky's concept or in Enzensberger's scenarios of a 'molecular civil war'[54] or in Trutz von Trotha's references to 'neo-Hobbesian wars'.[55]

Of course, the problems and inadequacies of these synthetic concepts for the new wars point not so much to defects in the authors' theoretical formation as to the obscure nature of recent trends that makes it almost impossible to sum them up in a coherent concept, not to speak of an actual theory.[56] Dramatic changes in weapons technology and the computerization of the battlefield are characteristic developments, but another characteristic is the return to archaic forms of violence practised mostly with firearms but often only with knives or machetes. On the one hand, we see an ideologization of violence drawing mainly upon religious sources, which many Western intellectuals wish to end through an educative dialogue; yet it can scarcely be denied that a large number of players in the new wars quite calculatingly pursue their interests by means of violence and, if necessary, use ideologies to legitimize their struggle. And finally, at a time when societies are being ethnically split into ever smaller units, there is also talk of new global political blocs constituted through religious cultures stretching across frontiers. Since the end of the East–West conflict, political constellations are more fragmented and contradictory than ever, and within them war occupies a new function that is clearly different from the one it had in earlier constellations and can scarcely be pinned down in a single concept. This is not the least of the reasons why – in discussions of intra-state

and transnational wars, and of terrorist strategies or military intervention to destroy the logistical bases of terrorist organizations –
people refer to 'new wars' without any further specification.[57] But,
of course, whether everything in them is as new as the comparison with classical inter-state war suggests will have to be further
considered.

Global political asymmetries and strategies to bring about asymmetry

First, we must take a closer look at an aspect that has long been
mentioned only in passing: the asymmetry of global political constellations. This has become more and more clear since the 1980s
and became definitive with the collapse of the Soviet Union. The
political-military conditions under which inter-state wars became
the principal and soon exclusive form of warfare in early modern
Europe were marked by the dominance of symmetrical relations –
indeed, we may say that inter-state war was the most developed form
of symmetrical warfare because it was comprehensively institution-
alized through legal regulation. Theoretically equal adversaries recognized each other in their equality, and this mutual recognition
underpinned a political rationality which might lead to arms races
but also to arms limitation agreements or partial disarmament. The
international rules of war, which are still valid today, also rested
upon this recognition. But these constellations, in which temporary
imbalances between the powers were repeatedly evened out before
they grew into manifest asymmetries, have become a thing of the
past. No state on earth, not even a coalition of states, can today challenge the United States on a military level. The disproportion begins
with aircraft carriers and air forces, continues through satellite reconnaissance and laser-guided bombs and ends with nuclear weapons
and missile systems.

If one uses the model of symmetrical warfare and inter-state wars,
no other power is even close to being a match for the United States.
Things look quite different, of course, if these asymmetrical constellations are in turn answered with strategies to bring about asymmetry.
Strategies of this kind are guerrilla warfare and terrorism. But they
also include what has become known from the Palestinian conflict
as intifada:[58] attacks by stone-throwing youths on heavily armed
soldiers, the attacker's only protection being the press cameras that
make the uneven conditions of the struggle known throughout the

world. What tanks and semi-automatics are for soldiers, TV crews are for these young people – stones being used, if necessary, to capture their attention.

The impotence of military apparatuses in the face of asymmetrical strategies was first brought home to the United States during the Vietnam War, when its vast technological superiority in weaponry was incapable of decisively defeating a guerrilla-style enemy. Two decades later, the Soviet Union had a similar experience in Afghanistan. And the vulnerability of the United States became even clearer in Lebanon and Somalia: a bomb devastated a US marine barracks in Beirut and a failed attempt to arrest the Somali warlord Aidid led to heavy American casualties. Pictures of a mutilated American soldier being dragged through the streets of Mogadishu led Washington to pull its troops out in short order and to accept before the eyes of the world that it could no longer enforce its political will. The so-called Mogadishu effect soon meant that US military threats lost a great deal of their credibility, and the USA found itself suspected (and therefore held in contempt) for having succumbed to the post-heroic mentality of a consumption and luxury society. David Rieff reported the scornful remarks of one Bosnian Serb:

> You think the American public was upset when eighteen of your soldiers were killed in Africa. Wait until the coffins start coming back from Bosnia. You are not a strong nation anymore. You cannot stand the idea of your children dying. But we Serbs can look at death. We are not afraid. That is why we will beat you even if you come to help these Turks [i.e. the Bosnian Muslims] you love so much.[59]

Since the United States had to do something to make up for the loss of face, it was forced to display greater determination in a number of subsequent conflicts than its political line would otherwise have required. Above all, however, the Mogadishu experience evidently confirmed Osama bin Laden's belief that, despite their technological superiority, the Americans could be defeated through a resolute use of force. In 1997, in an interview with the Middle East correspondent of the London *Independent*, he said that his people had been surprised how quickly the Americans gave up Somalia: 'The Mujahedin were amazed at the collapse of American morale. It convinced us that America is a paper tiger.'[60]

So, the message from Beirut and Mogadishu, eagerly taken up by the enemies and opponents of the USA, was that the world's mighty superpower was vulnerable – especially when it was fought on other

Defiled corpse of a US soldier in Mogadishu, 1993
The new warlords generally have little with which to answer the technological superiority of Western troops – except for pictures showing what will
happen to a soldier who falls into their hands. Pictures such as this one of
the defiled body of a US soldier in Mogadishu are weapons in themselves,
directed against the political will of a country that sends its troops into crisis
regions or war zones. Photograph: Ullstein.

fields and with other means than those traditionally associated with war. The media acquired growing importance, for they brought to the American public the images with which militants around the world sought to influence the decisions of its government. This new dimension began at one end with the commissioning of publicity agencies to improve the public image of certain countries, and ended with hostage-taking or the execution of American citizens by terrorist groups, the sole purpose being to make news in the Western media. This image warfare increasingly cut across the armed struggle, and considerably increased the effectiveness of terrorist strategies in particular.[61] In any event, the use of images of war as a method of war – the transformation of war reporting into a reporting war – represents a huge step in the asymmetrization of war. And, since pictures have long been used to make a population less willing to support and follow the political decisions of its government, the control and censorship of images has become an instrument in repelling attacks on those decisions.

The history of war since the middle of the twentieth century may thus be seen in terms of a rising trend in the asymmetrical pursuit of conflicts. The emergence of global political asymmetries, due to the impossibility of matching the economic, technological, military and culture-industry superiority of the United States, goes together with an asymmetrization of war through the moving of battle zones, the redefinition of combat methods and the mobilization of new resources. A first major step in this direction was the systematic recourse to guerrilla strategy in the epoch of decolonization – including the use of terrorist tactics, as in the Algerian war from the late 1950s on. Eventually a political-military strategy took shape in which terrorist attacks no longer served simply to support a guerrilla-style liberation movement but directly served to shatter the political will of the enemy. This shift took place in stages – from the first spectacular hijacking in the late 1960s to the double attack of 11 September 2001 on the Pentagon and the World Trade Center. In the process, terrorism has gone more and more on to the offensive and gradually spread out from its original birthplaces to acquire a global reach. This offensive capacity has grown to the extent that terrorists have managed to increase the asymmetries in the perception and pursuit of conflicts. The latest stage in this asymmetrization came on 9/11, with the conversion of civilian passenger aircraft into flying bombs and of office skyscrapers into battlefields.

If we compare guerrilla warfare with terrorism, another aspect of recent developments leaps to the eye. Whereas guerrilla warfare is basically a defensive form of asymmetrization, designed for use against a militarily superior occupying power, terrorism is the offensive form of the strategic asymmetrization of force. Although its goals may be politically defensive or conservative, terrorism as a military strategy is characterized by the carrying of violence into the population centres of the enemy under attack. Guerrillas are not capable of doing that; they rely upon the support of the population in the areas where they operate. The offensive capacities of terrorists rest upon their logistical use of the civilian infrastructure of the country under attack, and at the same time on their conversion of it into a weapon.

Classical inter-state warfare, at least until the arrival of strategic bombing and the first nuclear attacks, was waged between two armed forces in accordance with the principles of symmetry. Guerrilla warfare, on the other hand, aims to undermine the economic or political staying power of the enemy, on the assumption that, if the human casualties increase and the economic damage grows ever more burdensome for the colonial or occupying power, that power will become more willing to consider a so-called political solution involving the withdrawal of its troops. To succeed, then, guerrillas do not have to win militarily but only to maintain a constant threat. Raymond Aron, one of the sharpest and most intelligent observers of twentieth-century war, early realized the effect of this asymmetry. In a formulation that was later much quoted, and varied, he argued that so long as guerrillas do not lose militarily they will win the war politically, whereas if their opponents do not achieve a decisive military victory they will lose the war politically and militarily. In a war, then, it is guerrilla forces that have time on their side.[62] So long as they are not wiped out militarily, the costs they inflict will be so great in the long term that the other side will want to end the war.

The strategy of terrorism drives this asymmetry up a further notch. Unlike guerrilla warfare, it does not *indirectly* target the staying power of a population, but rather *directly* attacks it through acts designed to inspire terror. Terrorists thus deliberately exploit the effects produced by the media spotlight on their actions. Terrorism and guerrilla warfare differ from each other not only in their offensive or defensive character, but also because the latter generates asymmetries through the *slowing down of war* and the former through its *speeding up*.

The asymmetries that have emerged in the last few decades are not, however, limited to military strategies but have also affected the political rationality and international legitimacy of war and preparations for war. Under conditions of symmetrical war, such as those which marked modern European history, the political rationality of sovereigns and their executives was bound up with symmetry. The raising of armies, the forging of alliances and all the other measures undertaken to prepare for or avoid future wars were not geared to the strength of an actual or potential enemy. Since the same kind of weaponry was used on both sides, a stable balance of arms and men tended to exist or could be created through a rearmament drive. This was still true during the forty years of the East–West conflict, when the two military blocs guided themselves by the strength of the other side in signing arms limitation agreements and in periodically launching, or responding to, new weapons programmes. This is no longer the situation today. Now the United States arms by itself,[63] without the measure of a symmetrical adversary such as the Soviet Union was until 1991, and with reference only to danger scenarios essentially characterized by asymmetrical strategies.

Finally, the asymmetry of political rationality is continued and intensified in an asymmetry of international legitimacy. Whereas, after the seventeenth century, international law was in principle the same for all European states – in the sense that each was recognized as a sovereign power with the right to declare war (*ius ad bellum*),[64] it cannot be argued that things are the same today. The revival of the idea of just war, which had been largely driven from the interstate legal order,[65] is the clearest evidence of change in this area too. Whoever claims to be waging a *just* war already believes that the legal entitlements of the two adversaries are asymmetrical: one has all the right on its side, the other all the wrong. The model is that of the criminal who must be rendered harmless by police action and, once arrested, brought before the courts. Or else, in a kind of ratcheting up of penal conceptions, the adversary becomes an incarnation of evil who must be wiped off the face of the earth. Such notions are especially present where religious fundamentalism has made its way into politics. Just war and holy war stand opposed to each other as mirror images.[66] They constitute a symmetry of asymmetries, as it were.

Our initial survey has shown that two main features differentiate the new wars from the inter-state wars of the past: first, the phenomena of privatization and commercialization, and therefore the involvement of private players driven more by economic than by political motives; and second, the development of a new asymmetry – that is, the clash of military strategies and political rationalities which are in principle dissimilar from each other, and which, all recent efforts notwithstanding, escape regulation and limitation by international law. There is much to suggest that this trend has by no means reached its peak.

Such is the situation today. Let us first ask how it came about.

2

WARFARE, STATE BUILDING AND THE THIRTY YEARS' WAR

What can Clausewitz still help to explain?

There is a widespread idea that the wars of the last twenty or thirty years in South East Asia, Central Asia and especially Black Africa have little significance for the rest of the world – above all for the OECD countries. Politically, they are regarded as wars on the periphery of the zones of prosperity and stability that need trouble us only in exceptional circumstances; historically, they are seen as a type of war that Europe has long since left behind; and, last but not least, the frequently heard allusion to their religious or ethnic roots is supposed to confirm the belief that they belong to our past, not our future.

Some time ago, in resolute opposition to this way of thinking, the sociologist Trutz von Trotha took the view that the wars associated with the collapse of the state in Africa pointed to the future rather than the past of the OECD world.[1] In keeping with the trend, the Israeli military historian Martin van Creveld has come to a similar conclusion: that the epoch of inter-state wars, as it was paradigmatically recorded and analysed in Clausewitz's work, has come to a definitive end, and that we have entered a new epoch in which 'low-intensity wars' can keep smouldering for a long period of time.[2] Van Creveld's choice of vocabulary already conveys the radical nature of the changes. Wars are no longer conducted but *smoulder on*. Indeed, the position of war as the subject of sentences suggests that it is no longer simply an instrument of politics (as Clausewitz would have had it[3]) but has actually put itself in the place of politics:

No war is commenced, or, at least, no war should be commenced, if people acted wisely, without first seeking a reply to the question, What is to be attained by and in the same? The first is the final object; the other is the intermediate aim. By this chief consideration the whole course of the war is prescribed, the extent of the means and the measure of energy are determined; its influence manifests itself down to the smallest organ of action.[4]

Of course, this is only partly true of the new wars, which are neither begun nor ended; or, as nearly all observers of recent wars have noted, they begin *somehow or other* and end *somewhere or other*. Scarcely any of the parties involved can say clearly and precisely which purposes and aims are being pursued by means of the war. To exaggerate a little: the new wars conduct themselves; those who take part in them are conducted.

Clausewitz objected to scarcely any other view as vigorously as he opposed the idea that war obeyed a logic and laws of its own:

We maintain, on the contrary, that war is nothing but a continuation of political intercourse, with a mixture of other means. We say mixed with other means in order thereby to maintain at the same time that this political intercourse does not cease by the war itself, is not changed into something quite different, but that, in its essence, it continues to exist, whatever may be the form of the means which it uses, and that the chief lines on which the events of the war progress, and to which they are attached, are only the general features of the policy which run all through the war until peace takes place. And how can we conceive it to be otherwise? Does the cessation of diplomatic notes stop the political relations between different nations and governments? Is not war merely another kind of writing and language for political thoughts? It has certainly a grammar of its own, but its logic is not peculiar to itself.[5]

This key passage from Clausewitz's main work, *On War*, has been quoted at such length because it concisely summarizes the guidelines and principles of inter-state war. It presents the folly that throws the specificity of the new wars into such sharp relief. Only in certain cases will it be possible to say that they are 'a continuation of politics by other means', and even then mostly in respect of intervention by foreign powers. Nor is it the case that they are attached to the general or basic features of policy, because as a rule there are no such general features. The new wars, one might say as a variation on Clausewitz, have not only a grammar but also a logic of their own. This finds expression in statements that contain war as their subject: War 'smoulders on', 'spreads out', 'extends over' and so on. If these are more than a mere manner of speaking, what they assume – and Martin van Creveld certainly does assume it – is that war as the subject of events will not stop at the frontiers of Europe and North America but will sooner or later move beyond them. Von Trotha thought so too when he argued that the wars in Black Africa pointed to Europe's future rather than its past. If this is true, then the recent Balkan wars and the terrorist attacks of 11 September 2001 are not marginal phenomena or one-off events, but must be seen as harbingers of future developments, as historical signs that concern us all.[6] Anyone who makes war the grammatical subject in their descriptive writing and analysis should be clear what they are thereby saying about the future. Any analysis that takes its implications even approximately into account must have considered proposals about how such a development can be prevented.

What can certainly be said is that, contrary to many hopes,[7] the prospect of an end to large wars is not synonymous with the dawning of perpetual peace but goes hand in hand with the spread of small wars.[8] Of course, the term small wars is meant to imply not that they are of short duration or cause little damage and few casualties, but that they are fought mostly with light weapons and only partly with regular armies. Over time, the destructive impact of small wars is at least as great as that of the classical large wars. The striking interest that cultural theorists have recently shown in war and violence might be another sign that war can no longer be understood as an instrument of policy,[9] in Clausewitz's sense, and that it has become an independent way of life or an act of heightened (male) self-expression.[10] But is that really the case? And can these isolated observations be knitted together into a theoretically coherent framework? If Clausewitz's formulation that war is the continuation of politics by other means no longer holds true, because there is little sign of policy goals in the new wars, then what appears in the place of politics? Or has politics merely detached itself from its state form, without disappearing completely?

Military decisions and the art of policy demarcation

The confusion that the challenge of the new wars has caused among many researchers on peace and conflict issues suggests that it would be useful to look more closely at wars in the period before their statization – and not, to be sure, with any feeling of certainty that

Europe has totally left behind the combination of robbery and plunder, massacre and witch hunting that characterized many wars of the late Middle Ages and the early modern period. Indeed, the present confusion is a warning sign of what will happen to Europeans and Americans if they do not succeed in restoring (or asserting for the first time) the state's monopoly of violence at a global level, so that states become (or are again) the only lords of war.[11] In any event, a number of observers have been struck by the structural affinities between the new wars in Central Asia and Black Africa and the wars in Europe before armies were absorbed into the central state power. The wars of the late Middle Ages and, in part, the early modern period were conducted as expeditions against the enemy's estates and possessions. Since it was seldom possible to seize the enemy's strongholds, castles and walled cities, the aim was to devastate the surrounding countryside by attacking villages and burning down farms. Battles occurred only if the endangered prince went into action against the robber hordes instead of keeping out of their way. This was not very common, and so late-medieval warfare typically involved devastation more than armed encounters and battles. This is confirmed by an estimate of those killed in action as a percentage of total troop numbers: 4.6 per cent for the fourteenth century, 5.7 per cent for the fifteenth century, but then up to 15.7 per cent in the seventeenth century.[12]

This upward trend is usually attributed to the introduction of firearms, but just as significant were changes in the conduct of war. So long as battles were avoided and skirmishes were decided at the first deployment of armoured cavalry, the numbers killed in action were inevitably smaller than at a time when a resolution of war was sought on the battlefield and troops were trained and equipped to endure a protracted encounter with the enemy. Accordingly, tactics developed to ensure that forces could be used right through a battle, with the result that they became considerably bloodier. This does not mean, of course, that war in general took a greater toll in human lives. At first, all that changed were the place and mode of the application of force. The violence used by all the parties in the total space of the war was now concentrated on the battlefield.

Previously, those who suffered from the depredations of war were not so much the soldiery on either side (they conveniently kept out of the way) as the peasants, women and children, who were dragooned, plundered, raped and murdered.[13] The point of war was not to seize large areas from the enemy, to occupy or even annex them politically; most belligerents would anyway have been incapable of that, since they lacked both the troop strengths and the

Sebastian Vrancx, *Plundering a Village*, c.1620
In many respects, the new wars resemble those of the early modern period
rather than the inter-state wars of the last three centuries – especially in their
use of violence against the civilian population. Plunder, rape and massacre
mark them much more strongly than major or decisive battles. Photograph:
Archiv für Kunst und Geschichte.

funds to maintain an army for any length of time. Instead, the aim
was to inflict lasting damage on the enemy, thereby forcing them to
meet certain demands or to agree to a treaty. To put it in modern
terms, war was used to raise the price that the enemy had to pay for
maintaining (political) will, in the hope that they would be forced to
give way. As a rule, then, wars were fought not to break the enemy's
political will in battle, but to wear the enemy down by inflicting constant damage. Hans Delbrück – in a different context – has coined
the term 'exhaustion strategy' to describe this. And not a few of the
new wars may be understood as a return to forms of warfare that
aim at long-term damage rather than a speedy resolution. Use of the
term 'exhaustion strategy' to describe this kind of warfare does, of
course, assume that a recognizable political-military plan has led to
the deliberate adoption of this strategy. However, when it is said of
war that it smoulders on, there can be no talk of strategic directives.

    With the statization of war, direct confrontation between the two
armies in a decisive battle acquired much greater significance, even

though the 'supplies and exhaustion' war remained a strategic option that was repeatedly taken up. Inter-state wars favour a *military* resolution of the issues in contention, and the (whenever possible) decisive battle may be seen as a kind of complexity reduction in which the most diverse motives and objectives, interests and value combinations are bundled together and set off against one another in the military forces on either side. These forces join battle to clear away all outstanding problems and issues at a single stroke and for a long time into the future. 'The battle is the bloodiest way of solution', writes Clausewitz. And because it is the bloodiest way, it faces the commander with two challenges in particular. First, thousands of trusted soldiers must be sent to their death within the space of a few hours: 'True, it [the battle] is not merely reciprocal slaughter, and its effect is more a killing of the enemy's courage than of the enemy's soldiers . . . but still blood is always its price, and slaughter its character as well as name; from this the humanity in the General's mind recoils with horror.' It is also associated with the much greater burden of having to make decisions which, in a few moments, can alter the fate of entire countries:

> The soul of man trembles still more at the thought of the decision to be given with one single blow. *In one point* of space and time all action is here pressed together, and at such a moment there is stirred up within us a dim feeling as if in this narrow space all our forces could not develop themselves and come into activity, as if we had already gained much by mere time. . . . This is all mere illusion, but even as illusion it is something, and the same weakness which seizes upon the man in every other momentous decision may well be felt more powerfully by the General, when he must stake interest of such enormous weight upon one venture.[14]

Clausewitz thought that this explained why commanders from different epochs had again and again sought to avoid 'the bloodiest way of solution' and to pursue victory by other means.

The prerequisite for the eventual transformation of warfare, from devastation of the enemy's lands to military resolution in a great battle, was a system of distinctions and demarcations such as only states could develop and enforce in the way that they did. The statization of war thus developed in parallel with the increase in the numbers of battles fought in war. The distinctions in question were the prerequisite for complex problems to be reduced to the *decisive military action*, and for this to be accepted as the *solution* of the issues in dispute. This is far from self-evident, as we may see from the new wars that drag on for long periods with no possibility of a military resolution. There are six distinctions and demarcations that the state performs and guarantees.

(1) The state sets recognized territorial boundaries that allow an inside and an outside to be precisely distinguished. This is the basis for the organization of the state apparatus – from the separation between internal and external policy through to the definition of the responsibilities of the police and military (at least in a constitutional state). Above all, however, the territorial borders mark out the sphere in which orders and expectations of obedience are legally binding, or at least enforceable. Such precise boundaries differentiate states from those empires whose claim to rule diminishes as it moves outward from centre to periphery, not ending at any frontier line but losing itself in the depths of large frontier regions.

(2) This territorial demarcation makes it possible to distinguish clearly between war and peace; precise boundaries are the prerequisite for there to be no intermediate status between war and peace. Unless those on guard give their permission, any crossing of a frontier is a violation of the peace and may become a reason for war. In the border zones of great empires, on the other hand, it was often impossible to distinguish reliably between war and peace. What prevailed there was an intermediate situation, which could not be described as either war or peace. For centuries this was true of the eastern and south-eastern fringes of the Tsarist Empire, the border regions of the Ottoman Empire, and the so-called Military Frontier of the Austro-Hungarian Empire; it applied to nearly all the border regions of the European colonial empires and to the West and South of the United States, before settlers reached the Pacific Coast or a state frontier was established with Mexico. In all these regions, acts of warlike violence were always on the cards, even when the realm was officially at peace. There were no neighbours of like nature, or recognized as equals, with whom binding treaties and agreements could be signed, and so the empires tried to secure their frontiers by settling there whole peoples or groups of volunteers who would be constantly prepared to fight. Jürgen Osterhammel has coined the term 'imperial frontier with the barbarians' to describe this kind of region.[15] Anyone who settled there was mostly aware of the special dangers. Citizens of a state, by contrast, even if they live in an area close to the frontier, are confident of being able to enjoy the blessings of peace during periods when it officially prevails. Many loci of the new wars are exceptions, however: they appear to be global excrescences of the border regions of the old empires. And the wars

prevailing there mostly have nothing in common with the inter-state wars of early modern Europe.

(3) The binary coding of aggregate political conditions as either war or peace is supplemented by the state's exclusive claim to define who, in a political sense, is to count as a *friend* and who as an *enemy*.[16] The relationship of vertical loyalty under feudal law was thus turned into the demand for horizontal loyalty by the territorial state, and anyone who ignored this change was tried and punished for high treason.[17] The sovereign's decision as to who was a friend and who was an enemy was binding on all his subjects. In the new wars, on the other hand, a local warlord – or often just an individual checkpoint – decides whether someone is to be treated as friend or enemy.

These are the three basic distinctions and demarcations on which the modern territorial state rests (in contrast to the state of the Middle Ages or antiquity, which had its foundation in personal ties). But there are also three further distinctions or demarcations, of varying importance for the legal form of the state and the clarification of inter-state relations.

(4) There is the distinction between combatants and non-combatants, that is, between those who, identifiable as members of the armed forces by their clothing (since the seventeenth century: uniform) and their bearing of weapons, may be attacked and killed, and all others, who, since they do not take part in fighting and have no say in military decisions, may be neither robbed nor killed. The protection of non-combatants from the effects of war became possible with the previously mentioned transition from a strategy of economic damage to a strategy in which battle determined the outcome of war. Battle thus invariably has a symbolic aspect inscribed within it: the destruction of power symbols, which nearly always occurs in a battle, overlies and complements the physical fighting and lends a definitive meaning to victory or defeat. Without this symbolic dimension, the outcome of many battles would not necessarily have resulted in the end of the war and the signing of a peace treaty. Inter-state war is sensitive to the symbolism of defeat; the new wars are not – which is another reason why they last so long. Whereas the warfare of plunder and destruction mainly targeted civilian populations, the violence of inter-state war theoretically affected combatants alone. Granted, this was true only of the *large war*; the *small war* accompanying it was still intended to inflict considerable damage on civilians. With the statization of war, the new type of warfare did not completely displace

the old but downgraded it, precisely as small war, to the role of a strategic aid.[18] In a way, the new wars may therefore be described as an autonomization of small war in relation to large war. This goes hand in hand with a loss of political symbolism: the collapse of a state is always also a collapse of political symbols, and their loss forces a physical resolution.

(5) At least with regard to large war and regular troops, the state was able to draw a clear dividing line between the permissible violence of acts of war and criminal violence. This concerns both the distinction between war and peace and the delimitation of permissible violence in war. The quartering of troops in barracks (where they were subject to stricter control and discipline than in field camps), together with the introduction of courts martial to replace the peer-group courts common in landsknecht contingents, had a major civilizing effect upon public life.[19] It brought to an end the age of the 'roving' landsknecht, who had wandered the land searching for employment, robbing, plundering and raping along the way. Beggars, outcasts and criminals had often joined their ranks, and their eventual separation from the army proper made it much easier to enforce law and order than when landsknecht mercenaries had threatened it in groups a hundred or even a thousand strong.[20] Eventually restrictions were also placed on the permissibility of violence in war. Article 22 of the Hague Land War Convention, adopted in 1907, states: 'The right of belligerents to adopt means of injuring the enemy is not unlimited.' And Article 3 of the Geneva Convention relative to the Protection of Civilian Persons in Time of War, which came into force in October 1950, is even more precise: 'Persons taking no active part in the hostilities, including members of armed forces who have laid down their arms and those placed hors de combat by sickness, wounds, detention, or any other cause, shall in all circumstances be treated humanely, without any adverse distinction founded on race, colour, religion or faith, sex, birth or wealth, or any other similar criteria.[21] Thus, the distinction between violence in war and war crimes ultimately rests upon the capacity of the state to differentiate clearly between combatants and non-combatants. That states have themselves repeatedly ignored this distinction is beyond doubt,[22] but that is quite another matter from the collapse of the whole regulatory system which has accompanied the collapse of states and the emergence of the new wars.[23]

(6) As far as European economic development is concerned, the most important demarcation was probably that between the use of force

and commercial activity, which resulted in the closure of open markets in violence.[24] Instead of a soldiery recruited on an ad hoc basis, standing armies appeared which, even in peacetime, were armed and supplied by the state.[25] The armed power of states was thus no longer subject to the amortization logic of invested capital, but, right down to the twentieth century, was funded out of a tax-covered budget in which military expenditure represented notoriously high sums. However heavy and burdensome the taxation, the new system for the organization of military affairs had the great advantage that it removed the supply and demand of violence from the labour market and restricted the latter to civilian activity.[26] For the landsknecht-turned-soldier, this obviously meant that wages fell over the long term.[27] What literature often terms the militarization of politics initially led to a civilizing of society, since it largely prohibited the use of violence as a means of appropriating goods and services. To a considerable extent, violence was confined to the garrisons in which troops had their quarters, and even turned against them in the form of new disciplinary regulations, military drill and an extremely harsh set of punishments.

Of course, it took quite a long time for the modern territorial state to implement the distinctions and demarcations outlined above; the process began in the fifteenth century and reached completion only in the eighteenth century. Moreover, it did not develop everywhere at the same time or to the same degree. On the eastern periphery of Europe, in Poland and Russia, it was never consistently implemented, but was partly broken off or completely abandoned. As a result, Poland disappeared from European history for more than a century, while Russia's imperial expansion to the east and south also exposed it to other challenges than those of European-style state building. In the centre of Europe, in parallel with the state-building process, a principle of symmetry developed through a balance of powers that required states to catch up with one another in terms of modernization. Efficiency-raising distinctions and demarcations in one country forced its neighbours to keep pace by making similar efforts of their own. To this extent, the development of a symmetrical warfare system and the emergence of territorial states were mutually reinforcing processes, interrupted only by the great crisis of the Thirty Years' War and its massive backsliding into forms of warfare that had already been overcome. It therefore seems likely that a closer look at the Thirty Years' War will yield some valuable hints about the structural principles and development dynamics of the new wars since the end of the twentieth century.

The Thirty Years' War as an analytic framework and comparative reference for the new wars

The series of campaigns and wars between the years 1618 and 1648, which soon went down in history under the synthetic name 'Thirty Years' War', unquestionably marked a decisive turning point in the development of Europe. Central Europe, in particular, would long continue to suffer from its consequences, which were more serious demographically, socially and economically than those of any other conflict until the Second World War.[28] The Thirty Years' War, mainly fought on the territory of the German Reich yet anything but a purely German affair, was characterized first of all by the use of force not only against the armed enemy but also – at times principally – against the civilian population. It began with plunder and threats of pillage to extort the money required to pay and supply the troops,[29] but there were more and more cases where often starving soldiers banded together in groups of irregulars to seize the few available resources.[30] It is true that major battles became more frequent in the course of the war, but none of them brought a definitive military outcome – either because the losers soon regained their original strength with outside help or through the mobilization of new forces, or because other European powers took over and filled the arenas of war with fresh troops.[31] Thus, not one of the thirty-three major and minor battles of the Thirty Years' War led to a military resolution.[32] The different sides in the war therefore increasingly pursued a strategy that aimed not at *military defeat* of the enemy but at its *economic exhaustion*, and often their only objective was somehow or other to supply and maintain their own forces. Great campaigns were launched to lay waste enemy land, resulting in a form of war characterized by small skirmishes and expeditions, plundering and extortion, ambushes and massacres.

Whereas at first the various commanders consciously planned this type of warfare, they increasingly lost control of the troops engaged in it. These troops were soon fighting on their own account and there were no limits to the cruelty of their violence against the civilian population. In the summer of 1622, the village priest in Echzell wrote of the soldiers of Christian von Braunschweig who were quartered there:

> It is impossible to utter the shameful things they did with womenfolk; hard though it is to believe, they do not even spare sixty- or seventy-year-olds. An honourable young widow here complains that she was raped by three soldiers one after the other, right in the middle of the

room, within sight of several women and her own and other children. And they so ruined another maid in a nearby village – there were up to ten of them – that a few days later she gave up the ghost. They have shamelessly abused the women they come across in fields or gardens.[33]

The acts of cruelty became more frequent in the course of the war, as reasonably disciplined troops turned into marauding ruffians who plundered and murdered their way across the land.[34]

The capture and destruction of Magdeburg in 1631, by forces under the imperial commander Tilly, became a symbol of the uncontrollable behaviour of troops who, not having received any pay, no longer listened to their leaders' commands but gave free rein to greed and bloodlust. The Jesuit Gaspard Wiltheim from Luxemburg, who accompanied the forces of the Catholic League, reported the conditions in the city soon after its fall:

On the way I warned the soldiers accompanying me to respect the women's honour, as Tilly had ordered, and to refrain from killing people. Unfortunately, however, the streets were already strewn with dead bodies and the clothes of those who had been robbed. No consideration had been shown for women's honour. In front of the Peterskirche lay a heap of violated and murdered women. Our victorious landsknechts hurled themselves with dog-like lust upon the women of the vanquished city. This lecherous behaviour turned our victorious armies into bands of defeated men. They transformed the previous triumphs into permanent routs. Not only the ordinary landsknecht but even the officers besmirched themselves with this ignominy. Not content with one day's outburst of violence, they kidnapped the women they had violated and lugged them around for their further depravation.[35]

Wiltheim described the savagery during the capture of Magdeburg in order to explain the subsequent turn in the course of the war. For that episode brought to an end the victorious advance of the troops of the emperor and the Catholic League; heavy defeats followed at Breitenfeld and Lützen, and for a long time the Swedish-led coalition of Protestant powers gained the upper hand. But lack of discipline, resulting not least from supply problems, increasingly made itself felt in the Swedish ranks too. When large parts of the Frankish–Bavarian peasantry offered resistance to the continual plundering and violence and began to attack and kill marauding soldiers[36] ('freebooters, highwaymen and brigands', as they were called), the Swedish troops took their revenge by reducing several

Hans Ulrich Franck, *Peasants Killing a Soldier*, 1643
In the course of the Thirty Years' War, civilians were subject to ever wors-
ening violence on the part of marauding soldiers. Hard-pressed peasants
increasingly turned to self-help, ambushing small troop units and killing
stragglers, whose comrades would then exact the most terrible revenge.
Photograph: Bildarchiv Preussischer Kulturbesitz.

hundred villages to rubble and ashes.[37] In Grimmelshausen's *Der
abenteuerliche Simplicissimus*[38] and Moscherosch's *Geschichte Philanders von Sittewald*,[39] as well as in the engravings of Caillot and
Franck, atrocities are represented from precisely this phase of the
war. Grimmelshausen, in particular, depicted war as a form of rap-
ine directed against the civilian population[40] – a routinization of
violence in which it is no longer clear what contribution it makes to
military victory.

Wars that are not intended to secure a swift military resolution
nearly always end in the loss of discipline. The men under arms
increasingly go over to using war as a means to personal enrichment and guns as an instrument for the acting out of fantasies of
omnipotence and sadism. It is in this respect that the similarities are
so striking between reports from the Thirty Years' War and recent
trends. But a structural parallel with the new wars is also apparent

in the war economy organized according to the principle of *bellum se ipse alet* (war feeds war). Here, although state loans may make it possible to keep on fighting, there are no national reserves derived from tax revenue which define for how long and with what intensity the war may be conducted and therefore when it must come to an end. Instead, war itself becomes part of an economic life that is no longer under political control or subject to political limitation. To be sure, even under such conditions a war cannot last forever. As a one-sided appropriation of economic values, it creates no value itself and eats so deeply into the economic structures that total collapse is the eventual result. Nevertheless, since these wars do not usually involve a rapid and total mobilization of forces but slowly use them up on an ongoing basis, most of them last a long time and keep flaring up after temporary lulls.

Soon, private or semi-private operators appear in the place of civil servants and command staff. This was also true of the organization of the Thirty Years' War, which saw the participation of an estimated 1,500 small-scale and large-scale military entrepreneurs.[41] Albrecht von Wallenstein, Ernst zu Mansfeld, Christian von Braunschweig and Bernhard von Weimar are only the best known of these figures. Unlike certain condottieri in fifteenth-century Italy, none of them managed to establish a permanent rule of their own – although many, such as Ottavio Piccolomini or Wenzel Lobkowitz, did achieve great riches and powerful political influence.[42] At first, regiments were prepared for war by specially appointed colonels, who ran private businesses but were subject to state regulation. Soon, however, this initial framework lost more and more of its importance, and the actual conduct of war became autonomous of any political directives.

Nevertheless, this war could not have lasted for thirty years in Germany if new reserves had not continually flowed in from abroad – in the shape of fresh troops (most notably from Spain and Sweden as well as Scotland) and especially in the form of extra funds from England, France and the Netherlands. These subsidies prolonged the war in two ways: by making its continuation possible and by making its termination more difficult. The peace agreements were supposed to stipulate who was liable for the repayment of this money, and of course no one was capable of it any longer. Another point that we should bear in mind is that, without the constant flow of gold and silver from the New World and the emergence of world economic ties since the discovery of the Americas, it would have been difficult to sustain the war over a period of thirty years.

In principle it seems obvious – although it is usually overlooked or given too little attention – that wars normally last the longer the more access the participants have to the resources of the world economy. This was already true of classical inter-state wars. As a rule, the access to additional resources – certain raw materials, but especially weapons and money – is organized by the states of other countries; most of the peripheral wars at the time of the East–West conflict were fuelled and sustained in accordance with this model. Under conditions of globalization, however, which escape the control of individual states, the belligerents have unhindered access to the resources of the world economy. Thus, the so-called surrogate wars – which were at least partly controlled by the American and Soviet superpowers – have given way to ever more autonomous wars, whose duration depends not on the achievement of political goals but on the availability of further resources. If they eventually come to an end, they do so not because one side has attained its objectives but because each side is too exhausted to continue fighting. In this respect, too, the new wars have resemblances with the Thirty Years' War.

Officially, the Thirty Years' War ended in the autumn of 1648, through the two peace agreements of Münster and Osnabrück. But the fact that the negotiations took place at two different places, and that several parties took a long time to endorse the agreements, already indicates that we should speak of a peace *process* rather than a peace *settlement*.[43] Although the parties started conferring in the middle of 1645, and although political soundings were made at various levels, it took three years for the negotiations at Münster and Osnabrück to end in an agreement on the main (not all) points. This was partly due to the fact that many interest groups had taken shape in the course of the war and they could not be immediately pacified by the conclusion of the peace negotiations – above all, those for whom peace would mean the loss of their existing livelihood. It was clear that money would have to be found to solve the problem of the 'retirement of the warring peoples' – or anyway some 150,000 soldiers – but it was not clear who would actually provide it. Moreover, no military resolution had determined in advance the structure for the negotiations, and the involvement of many outside powers in the war had associated it with a number of other wars. In principle, four European wars had to be ended at Münster and Osnabrück if a stable and sustainable peace was to result in Germany: the war between France and Spain (here, of course, the peace talks failed); the war that had been dragging on for eighty years between Spain and the Northern low countries; the war between France and part of the Estates of the Empire; and the war between the emperor and part of the Estates plus Sweden. For some fourteen years there had been talk of holding a comprehensive European peace congress, before this finally resulted in the Peace of Westphalia. In comparison, the European inter-state wars of the eighteenth and nineteenth centuries, and even the First World War (which left a host of problems unresolved), were brought to a distinctly speedy end. Certainly the treaties concluded in 1919 in the Paris suburbs of Versailles, Saint-Germain, Trianon, Neuilly and Sèvres, often collectively known as the Paris Peace Conference, resulted in a peace that was considerably more fragile than those of Münster and Osnabrück – and for this reason the latter have increasingly been held up in recent years as masterworks of negotiation and statecraft.[44] What is too little appreciated, however, is that the war continued for many years after it had become clear that none of the belligerents had the military means to end it advantageously.

The Thirty Years' War, then, turns out to have involved a sequence and superimposition of several different wars and conflicts, so closely intertwined or interlinked that it is possible to speak of a single war.[45] This is another likeness it shares with a series of present-day wars. First, there is the *war in Afghanistan*, which actually consisted of a series of wars involving different parties. The devastating long-term consequences were similar to those of the Thirty Years' War in Germany: nearly a million dead (400,000 of them children) out of a total population of 13 million, 1.7 million war cripples and four to five million refugees.[46] Next there is the thirty-year war in *Angola*, in the course of which a little under 10 per cent of the population were killed and 20 per cent were forced to become refugees. Nearly three million Angolans are dependent upon aid from international organizations, and economic recovery, which will take years if not decades, will be especially difficult because of the 10 to 15 million landmines buried beneath the soil.[47] Then there is the *Congo War*, which up to now has claimed 1.7 million lives out of a total population of 30 million and created more than two million refugees. The presence of a number of rebel movements and outside powers meant that the Congolese war became entangled with other conflicts in the region, so that the prospect of a peace treaty keeps receding into the distance.[48] Finally, in the *Middle East*, the conflict between Israelis and Palestinians is intertwined with a number of regional wars, of which the one in Lebanon is the most protracted and the most fraught with consequences.[49] The list could be continued with reference to the Caucasus, the Horn of Africa and so on. All these wars have developed from intra-state conflicts into transnational conflicts, becoming literally *'sans frontières'*. It must therefore be considered a major success for the UN, NATO (North Atlantic

Treaty Organization) and the European Union that they geograph-
ically restricted the wars accompanying the collapse of Yugoslavia.
One of the most important future tasks of international peace policy,
in conditions where an early end to intra-state war is impossible,
will be to ensure that its transnationalization is at least seriously
impeded.[50]

The Thirty Years' War also began as an internal conflict, between
the Bohemian Estates and the emperor, but its links with the denominational confrontations of the time soon carried it beyond the
frontiers of Bohemia. Frederick V of the Palatinate and Maximilian
of Bavaria, who from the outset played a central role along with the
emperor, certainly did not become involved in the war solely because of their denominational allegiances (Calvinism in Frederick's
case, Catholicism in Maximilian's); they were also driven by personal
greed and power ambitions, the one being tempted by the Bohemian
crown, the other seeing the acquisition of the Palatinate Electorate
as the best way of advancing in the ranks of the Electors of the Holy
Roman Emperor. It would not be doing justice to the complex origins
of the Thirty Years' War to consider it purely as a religious war – and,
in fact, even in the earlier so-called Wars of Religion, especially those
in France, religious differences were by no means the only factor in
play.[51] Denominational affiliations and values certainly gave added
impetus to the war and made it more difficult to end – especially after
the emperor's Edict of Restitution in 1629, which gave Protestantism
in Germany reason to fear that there would be no political guarantees of its continued existence – but they were not the only causes
of the war. They were crucial to its extension across the frontiers
of Europe, but that extension would quite possibly have occurred
anyway.[52] Here again, we can see structural affinities with the new
wars, in which religious-ideological factors have seldom been the
true causes of the conflagration, even if they have often fanned the
flames.

It is certainly a truism that in war not only structures, institutions
and organizations are important but also leaders and organizers. In
intra-state wars, however, the latter have even greater significance
than in inter-state wars, since usually the institutions and organizations necessary for the conduct of the war have first to be created;
the presence or absence of charismatic leaders and brilliant organizers is of decisive significance for the war and for the peace. This is
clearly observable in the case of the Thirty Years' War. Wallenstein
certainly showed little evidence of charismatic qualities, and yet –
especially in conjunction with the banker Hans de Witte – he proved
an outstanding military organizer who also had considerable tactical

and strategic abilities. Without him the war would have gone differently; this immediately became clear when the emperor thought for a time that he could dispense with his services. Gustavus Adolphus, on the other hand, had charismatic qualities in a high degree. This was apparent not least in the way he led his troops and fought battles: again and again he would appear in the front ranks or in the midst of his army, urging them on to greater efforts or leading a fresh attack. Without him Sweden would scarcely have joined the war at all.[53] And, finally, at least the second phase of the war would have taken a different course if the man in charge of French policy had been not Cardinal Richelieu but someone whose actions were guided less by reasons of state and more by religious connections.[54] Apart from these outstanding figures, for whom personal advancement, shared religious values and reasons of state were dominant motives for action, numerous charismatic individuals played a decisive role in the second rank of leaders. Ernst zu Mansfeld, Christian von Braunschweig, Bernhard von Weimar and others were capable of reshaping their armies after major defeats; they replaced weapons lost on the battlefield, enlisted fresh support and reported back to the theatres of war.[55] Today the infrastructure of the new wars exhibits similarly charismatic entrepreneurs who, with the help of politicians from outside (perhaps more geared to general values or the interests of their own state), acquire influence and staying power, and for whom war is less a means of asserting long-term policy goals than a way of obtaining personal power and riches.

By virtue of all these aspects, the Thirty Years' War presents itself much more strongly than all later wars – the two world wars and the wars of liberation or pacification during the winding up of the old empires – as a comparative reference for analysis of the new wars. A further reason why this is so is that the Thirty Years' War took place when the statization of the social-political order was not yet complete, so that it involved the conflict and cooperation among state, semi-state and private players which is also typical of the new wars today. From the very beginning its main actors, apart from rulers such as the emperor or the Imperial Estates, were the up-and-coming military entrepreneurs who organized mercenary forces and paid less heed to their client's instructions than to interests of their own. The personnel at their disposal consisted of professional landsknechts who had already served in various theatres of war, but increasingly also of members of the lower classes who were searching for ways to make a living, as well as adventurers who wanted to use war to make their fortune.[56] Finally, outside powers intervened more and more in the war in line with their own interests and possibilities, offering one side or the other legitimacy, money and weapons. Sometimes they also took a direct part in the war by sending men from their own armed forces. Thus, the Thirty Years' War was characterized by a jumbled array of constitutional conflicts and religious-ideological oppositions, private aspirations to wealth and power, reasons of state and ties based on shared values. Only in the rarest of cases are such wars capable of a military resolution.

3

THE STATIZATION
OF WAR

War as commerce: the condottieri
and their successors

In the vicinity of Castiglione Fiorentino, two Franciscans once came across the English mercenary leader John Hawkwood (or Giovanni Acuto), of whom Italians in the Florence region were extremely fond.[1] In their usual way, they greeted the highly regarded condottiere with a cheerful 'May God give you peace, *monsignore!*' and were all the more taken aback when Hawkwood answered with a dry 'May God take away your alms!' They wondered why he had wished such a thing when they had wished him nothing but good. 'How can you think you are saying something good', he asked, 'when you come and wish God to let me go hungry? Don't you know that I live off war and that peace would ruin me? And just as I live off war, you live off alms. So, the answer I gave was fully in keeping with your greeting.'

Franco Sacchetti's little story from the late fourteenth century succinctly disclosed the principles of warfare in the age of the condottieri: war had become a business, and battles a service performed for money. This led Karl Marx to describe the activity of mercenaries as a prefiguration of wage labour.[2] The legal basis for this kind of warfare was the *condotta*, a contract drawn up by legal experts between a client (a city or a prince) and a condottiere, which usually specified such details as the level of remuneration, the number of troops, the length of time for which they were to be deployed and the duties they had to perform. In Germany this practice persisted right down to the Thirty Years' War in the form of the landsknecht system,[3] in which the equivalent of the *condotta* was a so-called *Kapitulation*, which included the enlistment certificate, articles of war and an agreement on payment. In the eighteenth century the British East India Company was still using a similar model for its wars.[4] Condottieri warfare corresponded to the spirit of trade by barter: it rationalized and systematized the personal services that had previously been performed by vassals (in the feudal system of the Middle Ages) and by the armed citizenry (in the system of city militias). Personal duty to the lord or city was replaced with the impersonal relationship of purchase and barter, the raising of a city force gave way to the recruitment of professional fighters for a limited period, and the fealty obligation of the medieval vassal dissolved into a time contract mediated by money.[5]

This process opened up military affairs to society at large: the bearing of arms was no longer a privilege of the nobility but, in principle, an activity at which anyone could try their hand. After centuries in which powerful mechanisms of exclusion had been in play, the military sphere now became a springboard for social advance. Thus, in fifteenth-century Italy a series of condottieri even succeeded in climbing to the position of prince or duke through their victories on the battlefield. Francesco Sforza, who rose to become ruler of Lombardy, is the best-known and most successful example of this kind; but Bartolomeo Colleoni and Erasmo da Narni (known as Malatesta), Jacopo Piccinino and Francesco Bussone, later Count of Carmagnola, all came from modest circumstances and, at least for a time, achieved fame and honour, power and wealth.[6] The condottiere contingents were a happy hunting ground for adventurers seeking to make their fortune with arms, or to use their arms to make fortune bow to their will. The ranks soon filled up with soldiers of fortune.

But social advancement was not granted to all; considerable numbers died of epidemics or other diseases, and many who thought their heart's desire was within reach suddenly fell to the lower depths. The fate of Wallenstein, thrown to the wolves by an imperial client who suspected him of conspiring with the enemy, already had precedents among the Italian condottieri: Jacopo Piccinino fell into a trap laid for him by King Ferrante of Naples, who had him arrested and killed; Count Carmagnola was accused of treachery by the Venetians, tortured and finally executed on Piazza San Marco; Niccolò da Tolentino met a similar fate in Milan, as did Paolo Vitelli in Florence. These stories are scarcely surprising. When the only bond between the political leadership and the military has been bought with money for a limited period, it does not take long for suspicions to creep in.

Besides, since condottieri often turned their mind to the next contract before the old one had come to an end, it was easily thought that they might not complete it with the necessary care – and, of course, they might also deliberately prolong a war in order to keep their pay coming in. A rapid conclusion would certainly not have suited them, and the condottieri and their men usually had little inclination to risk life and limb for a temporary client. They therefore soon developed a kind of warfare that mainly involved strategic manoeuvring rather than pitched battles.[7] If a major encounter or even a pitched battle became unavoidable, it would be concluded with as few losses as possible and any prisoners were soon handed back for a suitable ransom. The political clients usually had to find the money for the ransom, so that they not only failed to achieve their goal but had to pay more than the original estimate for success.

Again and again, condottieri faced the accusation that they were not waging war with the necessary seriousness but were playing a game for which the city had to pay. As in Sacchetti's moral tale of Hawkwood and the two Franciscans, they 'often [treat] those who pay them worse than the enemy's soldiers. For, although they give the impression of fighting against one another, they actually get on better than with those who have taken them into their service, and it looks as if they have said among themselves: "You rob over there, because I'm going to rob here."'[8] Sacchetti concluded that cities should remain at peace and think three times before deciding to make war. Niccolò Machiavelli, for his part, recommended the dismantling of the condottiere system so as to bring military affairs back under *political* control. He therefore advocated a return to the ancient model of civic militias:

> If anyone supports his state by the arms of mercenaries, he will never stand firm or sure, as they are disunited, ambitious, without discipline, faithless, bold amongst friends, cowardly against enemies; they have no fear of God, and keep no faith with men. . . . In peace you are despoiled by them, and in war by the enemy. The cause of this is that they have no love or other motive to keep them in the field beyond a trifling wage, which is not enough to make them ready to die for you. They are quite willing to be your soldiers so long as you do not make war, but when war comes, it is either fly or decamp altogether.[9]

When Machiavelli wrote those lines, the Italian condottiere system had already suffered a number of devastating defeats. Against the French, Spanish and Germans who had invaded the country, condottieri had nothing to show for themselves after several battles, and they were handing Italy over to the troops of foreign powers for which it was the main theatre in the struggle for European hegemony. It is true that the invaders also used the services of bands of mercenaries – for example, the Swiss *Reisläufer* in the case of the French king in particular, or the German landsknechts deployed by the emperor – but both the *Reisläufer* and the landsknechts waged war in a different way from the Italian condottieri. Whereas the latter consisted of small mounted units which, despite the new role of money, preserved much of the knightly ethos of medieval warfare, the mercenary bands from the North were largely made up of foot soldiers who, being significantly cheaper than cavalrymen, could be hired in considerably larger numbers.

The fact that, unlike in previous centuries, infantry could now fight it out with armoured cavalry was mainly due to the tactical square formation developed by the Swedes and perfected by the German landsknechts.[10] Armed with long spears, the foot soldiers within the square or circle were capable of defending themselves on all sides against cavalry attack, and on the offensive they were able to mass together with such force that scarcely anything could withstand them. At the most, these formations could be broken by artillery placed right in front of them; if the serried ranks began to dissolve under fire, a cavalry attack might then be able to scatter them. But for the artillery to be effective and to escape being overrun itself, the enemy had to have foot soldiers of its own. This meant that only armies which possessed infantry as well as cavalry and artillery could conduct a successful campaign; battles were now decided not only by numerical superiority but also by superior capacity to combine the three types of weaponry. Major encounters and pitched battles thus acquired the ability to decide a war, and in the battles of Ravenna, Marignano and Pavia, for example, the campaigns of the hegemonic European powers played the decisive role in the clash of rival armies.[11] But the development of large armies and the combination of different kinds of weaponry made war an increasingly expensive business. The statement that anyone who wants to fight a war needs money, money and more money became ever more accurate as it passed from the lips of Count Campobasso to Gian Giacomo Trivulzio and Raimondo Montecuccoli.[12] In the end, such wars could be fought only by states which, on the basis of tax revenue that had been steadily rising since the fifteenth century,[13] were able to deploy sufficient funds for a long period of time, and which gradually succeeded in bringing war back under their political sway after it had become part of economic life under the condottieri. The size of the ruler's territory, the degree of centralization and the levels of tax revenue were now the crucial factors in European war.

Innovations in weapons technology and revolutions in tactics

In their attempt to gain control over war, states initially fell back on the system of military organization developed by the condottieri; they sought to influence the actual conduct of war only indirectly, through the steering of money flows, the selection of war entrepreneurs and the insertion of clauses into the contracts they signed with these entrepreneurs. Especially in Germany, this resulted in an army that combined military commercialism with the collective features of landsknecht organization.[14] First, there was the system of self-armament, whereby the landsknechts had to provide for their own weapons and clothing out of their own pay and enlistment fee. Subsequently, a distinctive landsknecht dress clearly marked out military society from civil society and permanently breached the corporate rules of the sartorial order.[15]

Only the introduction of soldiers' uniforms in the course of the seventeenth century put an end to the colourful appearance of the landsknecht. This 'uniformization' already made an outwardly visible statement that the state had brought military affairs under its direct control. All independent expressions of corporate military organization were eliminated, together with such landsknecht institutions as the collective administration of justice, the sharing out of income from war booty and the social organization of the baggage train, which represented something like a substitute homeland for the itinerant mercenaries and might afford them a degree of care in the event of their being wounded or – more probably – falling ill. In this independent culture of the military underclasses, women, in particular, occupied major functions, ranging from butlers through to prostitutes (the camp whores who worked under a female supervisor). Many landsknechts even brought along their wives and children, so that the baggage train often consisted of more than the ranks of combatants.[16] This travelling society, which also included gunsmiths and armourers, was the real centre of resistance to all attempts by the state to impose its discipline; war had truly become a way of life. The landsknechts and their followers formed a parasitic parallel society, a state within the state,[17] and had interests of their

Daniel Hopfer, *German Landsknechts*, 1460
The landsknechts of the fifteenth and sixteenth centuries formed a community with its own customs and laws. Their clothing, which defied all the
rules of the class order, was not the least of the aspects setting them apart
from the rest of society. Photograph: Bildarchiv Preussischer Kulturbesitz.

own that were rarely the same as the political objectives of the state
leadership.

Quite diverse motives eventually accounted for the direct statization of military affairs: Protestant circles, in particular, criticized
the immorality of the landsknechts and their bad influence on the
rest of society;[18] whereas the increased reception of Stoic philosophy
and associated military theories from antiquity found expression in
the philosophical-military writings that accompanied the House of
Orange's army reform.[19] All these ideas could take effect, however,
only because they found support in a series of technological inven-
tions and tactical revolutions in warfare which enabled highly disciplined bodies of troops to begin to master the European battlefields.[20]
Only far-reaching innovations in artillery, as well as in fortification
and siege warfare, gave the state its opportunity to assert direct control of military affairs; moral appeals and theoretical writings would
scarcely have been sufficient for the purpose.

However it may seem in a European perspective, the statization
of military affairs was anything but an automatic or even probable

process; its success rested upon a combination of factors that could not have been expected to occur in that particular form. Historians and social scientists in a Weberian tradition are especially prone to overlook the contingent nature of this development. Basing themselves on Weber's thesis of rationalization, they construct an evolutionary logic in which the passage from an autonomous mercenary structure to a statized military apparatus appears as a necessary development; the most they ever ask is *when*, not *whether*, it is completed.[21] The optimistic assumption that the new wars are state-building wars, such as those which occurred in early modern Europe, is essentially based on this Weberian view of history. What is regularly left out of account is that the introduction of heavy weapons and the disciplining of the troops were centrally important in the statization of war. The new wars, on the other hand, are typically fought with light weapons, and deployment of disciplined fighting units is rarely decisive in their outcome. One of the reasons for the failure of state building in the last few decades is probably that, unlike in early modern Europe, there has been no comparable pressure for the construction of a military apparatus capable of conducting war externally, so that officers have soon occupied themselves with the 'regulation of internal affairs'.

The state, then, broke up the corporate structures of the landsknecht associations, took away their privileges and subjected them to its own strict control. Instead of playing at dice or cards, soldiers in the camp were given rigid duties; they now had to perform the fatigue work – degrading in their eyes – which had previously been assigned to labourers brought along for the purpose or to a rural population forced into service. The inculcation of discipline continued with marching in step and training drill, a system of mechanical movements that standardized the manoeuvring of large bodies of troops and increased the rate of fire in frontline formations. The state also supplied a uniform ('the king's dress') to replace the splendid and imaginative landsknecht outfit. Finally, the itinerant society of the army camp and its hangers-on disappeared with the quartering of the troops in fixed accommodation, where a strict, not to say brutal, system of penalties placed corporal punishment on the agenda. The tightly drilled mercenary of the early eighteenth century no longer bore the slightest resemblance to the self-confident landsknecht of the sixteenth and early seventeenth centuries.[22] Whereas the landsknechts had asserted and usually imposed their interests, the soldier of the state army had nothing left but to desert. To become sole master of war, the state had first to become master of its military force.

As we have seen, not the least prerequisite of success had been in-novations in weapons technology, the most notable of which was the introduction of heavy artillery. Although it is true that late-medieval warfare had already used the cannon, improved casting techniques now made it possible to increase the rate of fire and the size of the load, while new kinds of gun carriage made artillery more mobile and, from the late fifteenth century, capable of being effectively de-ployed in siege warfare and on the battlefield.[23] With the help of this artillery, an army could promptly batter down (or force to sur-render before it came to that) a fortress or a mountain redoubt that had resisted its advance for weeks or caused its forces to split up. In this way, the offensive won back strategic weight from the defensive: victories in the grand style became possible, and this meant that the previously preferred war of devastation became less significant than war of conquest. To conduct a war of conquest, a commander had to be able to fight battles and not merely pillage and lay waste the enemy's territory – and for this he needed reasonably disciplined troops. War against the population on enemy soil turned into war against the enemy's forces, and the ever more frequent battles made it more important to have artillery.

As heavy artillery was the most cost-intensive equipment for the early modern army, it soon became the measure of the state's fiscal capability. At first, in order to avoid tying up large capital sums in cannon, most states put under contract an independent expert to train men in the use of artillery. These experts formed a kind of guild, which agreed to resist the state's clutches as strongly and effectively as possible. In the end, the state could break its power only by directly taking over the production and maintenance of cannon as well as the training of men to use it. Max Weber's point that the characteristically modern process of rationalization and bureaucratization took place essentially through the separation of workers from their working tools is more applicable to artillery than to any other category of weapon. Weber himself illustrated this with reference to artillery.[24] At the same time, artillery became the favourite branch for bourgeois careers within the army.

At a stroke, the development of artillery made traditional fortifi-cation techniques worthless. Previously these had involved building walls and towers as high as possible so that they could not be climbed by the enemy. But now the rule was that the higher the wall, the more easily it could be smashed with heavy cannon. Ramparts and sloping walls supported by earth banks were of some use against artillery, as were trenches and projecting bastions in which, or on which, de-fenders could set up their own cannon to cover a threatened sector with flanking fire. Costs soared for the construction of modern and effective defensive positions, and the cities that had previously paid for their own walls and towers could not afford the higher sums. The feudal nobility, whose castles and fortresses no longer offered protection from attack, were excluded from the first great arms race of modern times: the contest between artillery and fortification, in which only the sovereign could be a serious participant. Not only the advances in weapons technology, but also the defensive changes that they induced, fitted in with the efforts of the territorial state to assert a monopoly on war.[25]

The innovations in weapons technology went together with other new developments. Driven mainly by the reforms initiated by Maurice of Orange,[26] a process began in Europe in the early seventeenth century which would eventually shape ordinary foot soldiers into a tactically flexible infantry. The square, compact formations of the landsknechts turned into long lines, which not only presented less of a target for enemy cannon but were also better suited for the aiming of musket fire from one's own ranks. Crucial to this trend was the growing importance of firearms and the invention of the bayonet, which enabled the musketeer, when necessary, to turn himself into a pikeman. Originally, halberdiers were to be found among the thousands-strong square of spear-bearing foot soldiers, their task being to butcher the enemy with (short) halberds after its position had been overrun. Now, however, their place was increasingly taken by men with heavy muskets or light harquebuses who, incapable of defending themselves because of the slowness of their weapons, would take up position on the edges and flanks of the square and, after firing a round, quickly move back inside.

The invention of the bayonet already made it possible to increase the ratio of musketeers to pikemen, but advances in the speed of fire soon meant that the infantry switched over entirely to firearms and that pikemen disappeared from the battle ranks. A key factor here was the introduction of the so-called countermarch by William and Maurice of Orange, a system whereby infantrymen drawn up in ranks of four or five were able to fire off salvoes in quick succession: the first rank immediately marched back into the gap left as the next one moved forward to fire, and so on. To ensure that these movements were as precise and synchronized as possible under battle conditions, William of Orange adapted from ancient models a mechanics of movement and a language of command in which the appropriate turns, about-turns and wheels became highly formalized.[27] Apart from increasing the rate of fire, this also allowed the troops to be deployed in smaller units that were considerably more flexible

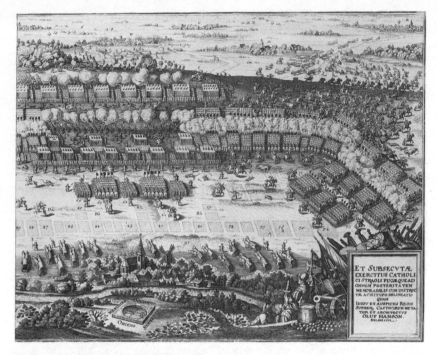

ET SUBSECVTÆ
EXERCITVS CATHOLI
CI STRAGIS FUGÆ QUEAD
OMNEM POSTERITATEM
MEMORABILIS CUM INSTRVC
TÆ ACIEI TYPO DELINEATIO
QUAM
IVSSV ET AVSPICIIS REGIS
SVPREM, CASTRORVM META
TOR ET ARCHITECTVS
OLVF HANSON.
DELINEAVIT.

Order of battle at Breitenfeld, 1631
At the beginning of modern times, battles ceased to involve simultaneous fighting among all the men under arms, but unfolded in a complex order that had to be carefully planned and precisely conducted by field commanders. As a rule, effective collaboration among the three forces – infantry, artillery and cavalry – decided victory or defeat. Photograph: Bildarchiv Preussischer Kulturbesitz.

for tactical purposes. In place of the four blocks in which the landsknechts had usually lined up, twenty-four battalions could now be deployed and moved around in several formations or lines of battle.

The state could not simply hire such an infantry on the European force markets, but had to maintain and regularly exercise it for years on end.[28] Soldiers became valuable because large sums had been invested in their training. And this was not the least of the reasons why the states of the eighteenth century, at a time when this military trend was reaching its peak, made every effort to prevent desertions and tried to incorporate or 'invest' already trained prisoners of war into the ranks of their own army. More than almost anything else, the development of a highly drilled line infantry in Europe contributed to the reliable separation of combatants from non-combatants – for anyone who had not spent years training to be a soldier was of no use in large-scale warfare. Undrilled (which literally meant undisciplined) fighters had their place only in small-scale warfare, where the barrier between combatants and non-combatants was shakier and more permeable. It is indeed scarcely surprising that, for all the efforts to define it precisely in international law, this distinction has been greatly eroded as small war has taken over from large war. International rules of war obviously cannot sustain that which has no safe and solid foundation in the social organization of military affairs. And so the recent attempts by legal theorists and social philosophers to develop and differentiate rules for most of the new wars have remained largely without effect;[29] they have acquired a certain significance only where Western democracies have in one way or another become embroiled in these wars. Michael Ignatieff has recently concluded that limits on violence against civilians are less likely to come from further legal regulation than from a revitalization of the old warrior's code of honour.[30]

The state as war monopolist and the development of European rules of war

At the time the state was developing its monopoly on war, the first requirements for anyone wishing to have a serious military apparatus at their disposal were a highly drilled infantry and a modern park of artillery – and only the territorial state was in a position to bear their dramatically increased costs. The war entrepreneurs, who had until then played a dominant role in the European force markets, were therefore excluded from what was actually no longer a business. Advance funding of a body of troops reasonably fit for battle now cost more than could be made from their later hiring out.[31] Yet, even if war itself was no longer a business, there was plenty of good business to be done from it: whoever wanted to turn a profit no longer raised troops but sold guns and other supplies to standing armies or else created factories to meet the ever-growing demand for weapons.

The capacity of the modern territorial state to fund these armies was anything but obvious; it derived only from the regularization and multiplication of tax revenue in the course of the fifteenth and sixteenth centuries. The state developed into a fiscal state, and the transition from occasional enlistment of fighting men to the establishment of a standing army went hand in hand with the transition from ad hoc taxation to a system designed to bring in a regular revenue.[32] Constant skimming of the social surplus product, and the building of a coercive apparatus to enforce this as and when necessary, were two parallel processes that determined and reinforced each other.[33] By enhancing the creditworthiness of the state, this regular income meant that the cyclical history of European war would now correspond to cycles of state debt. On the other hand, tax increases to service state loans repeatedly led to resistance: not only local revolts and uprisings but the great revolutions – the Dutch War of Independence, the English Revolution of 1640, the American War of Independence and the French Revolution of 1789 – in part had their origin in resistance to a tax burden that was experienced as arbitrary expropriation. Revolutionaries argued that, if it was unavoidable that the state should dip into people's pockets to ensure their security, the citizens themselves should at least have a say on matters relating to taxation. The fiscal prerogative of parliament imposed by these revolutions is not least a consequence of the vicissitudes of European military history.

The statization of military affairs and the state's monopoly on the right to declare and conduct war powerfully moulded relations between states. Based on the mechanisms of competition and the striving of larger countries for supremacy, a balance of power took shape in Europe which essentially involved the idea of symmetry.[34] Interstate wars in early modern Europe were, with a few exceptions,[35] fought as symmetrical wars, and this in turn made possible a special kind of legal regulation of war that did not develop anywhere else. Among the first casualties of this new symmetry was the old concept of just war, first outlined by Augustine of Hippo and Thomas Aquinas and further developed by Spanish neo-Scholastics of the Salamanca School.[36] However these various theories established whether a war was permissible or impermissible, they all concurred that one could speak of just war only when one side had broken the law and the other side was waging war to restore the rule of law. The right to wage war (*ius ad bellum*) was thus asymmetrically distributed: one party, so to speak, had all the right on its side. But certain rules of war (*ius in bello*) were still binding on that party; it was not allowed to engage in indiscriminate violence. Thomas Aquinas laid down three key criteria for a just war: sovereign authority (*auctoritas principis*), just cause (*causa iusta* – usually punishment of a wrong) and lawful intent (*intentio recta* – that is, war for the sake of peace and without the perpetration of atrocities).[37]

In the theory of just war, however, major restrictions on the use of force are generally of less significance than the political situation in response to which the theory was elaborated. Augustine, for example, directed his theory to a Christian community that was sworn to pacifism, his aim being to convince it that the Roman Empire must be defended against the migratory peoples pressing on it from all sides. As far as he was concerned, the purpose of just war was to preserve a status quo which, though certainly not entirely just, was still more just than any imaginable alternative. War was a conflict under basically asymmetrical conditions: on one side the Roman Empire, the political guarantor of a peaceful order and now also inspired by Christianity; on the other side, barbarian conquerors from whom only the worst was to be feared. Augustine's concept of just war thus served to justify the armed self-affirmation of a civilization against invading enemies of civilization. Much the same may be said of Thomas Aquinas's theory of just war, except that for him the place of the Roman Empire was taken by the political world of all Christendom and he also added elements of a military-humanitarian ethic of intervention.[38] The last great theorists of just war in Europe, the Spanish neo-Scholastics (Francisco de Vitoria, Domingo de Soto, Francisco de Suárez, Luis de Molina), also invoked the right of an ostensibly superior civilization to assert itself against others, even if this meant taking the offensive. They had to explain whether and to what extent it was legitimate to wage war against the inhabitants of the newly discovered world – especially if the purpose was to raise them to a higher level of civilization through conversion to Christianity. With their distinction between justified and unjustified force, the neo-Scholastics tried to curb the policy of violence employed by the conquistadors.[39] They almost completely failed to achieve this, of course: the Spanish conquerors continued to do what they wanted in Central and South America, without feeling hampered by the constructs of international law.

In general, the theory of just war is intended to empower and bond a superior (or in its own eyes superior) civilization against a 'savage' or 'barbarian' Other. It does not rest upon an idea of equality or sameness of the warring parties and is thus intimately related to the concept of Holy War to be found among various religions. In constructing asymmetrical situations to justify the use of force, both models differ fundamentally from theories which see war in terms of a duel or tournament between combatants of essentially the same nature, and which focus less on the grounds for starting a war than on the regulation and ritualization of violence between adversaries who respect each other as equals. The latter was in fact the direction taken by international law in Europe from the mid-seventeenth to the early twentieth century.

When this tendency began it was still under the sway of concepts of just war, so that the Italian legal theorist Alberico Gentili answered 'yes' to the question of whether a war could be just on both sides;[40] his formulation (*bellum iustum ex utraque parte*) expressed both the equality of the belligerents and the fact that neither side accepted any superordinate authority with the power to judge and settle the issues in dispute. If all parties considered capable of waging war recognized one another as equals – which the parties to the Treaty of Westphalia did recognize in principle – there could no longer be a further, higher position defined as different and unequal vis-à-vis the equal parties. Even the pope and the emperor, who had previously claimed such a position, eventually situated themselves on a level with other sovereign powers. The mutual admission of equality involved in the recognition of state sovereignty became the basis for Europe's international laws of war, according to which only sovereign states had the right to wage war. Since, moreover, no one else in Europe now had the capacity to wage war, this principle gained general acceptance there for several centuries.[41] States were permitted to wage war (*ius ad bellum*) without reference to a third party empowered to verify their grounds and claims. But they also had to follow certain formal procedures and had a strict obligation to observe the provisions and rules of international law (*ius in bello*), especially in relation to neutral powers and the sparing of combatants.

The idea that warring parties must respect the *neutrality of third parties* could appear in this form only after theories of just war had declined in importance. With the contemporary revival of such theories, however, the willingness to exercise restraint with regard to third parties has been disappearing. When war is fought to enforce the law, to assist the establishment of justice, neutrality becomes morally disreputable. The present war on terrorism, for example, does not acknowledge neutrality: in the words of the US president, whoever is not on the side of the United States is against it. As to the *sparing of combatants*, this means that soldiers must not regard their adversaries as illegitimate enemies, or their weapons and personal belongings as war booty. Even what does legitimately count as booty should be of only marginal interest to a soldier, since it belongs to the state, the holder of the monopoly on war, not to the troops in its pay. Legal regulation of warfare thus gives rise to legal regulation of the soldiery, who become (in Balthasar de Ayala's expression) *iustus hostis*, able to claim a certain number of rights, especially the right to life and property in the event of being wounded and taken prisoner.[42] The only protection formerly enjoyed by prisoners came from the fact that they were a material value, capable of being ransomed for a profit. When there was no prospect of a ransom, they were either killed or mutilated so that they could not take part in any future hostilities – a practice that is again increasingly visible in the new wars. International law, as it took shape in the modern age, stipulated that prisoners must not be maimed or tortured and that they could be executed only once proven guilty of war crimes by due legal process.

As the new provisions of international law gradually ended the practice of taking battlefield booty from the dead and wounded, it became strategically more feasible to follow up a victory by energetically pursuing the defeated enemy. Once the troops no longer halted to plunder on the field of battle, they could – as Clausewitz argued – give chase and thereby flesh out the victory. 'But under any conceivable circumstances the fact holds good, that without a pursuit no victory can have a great effect, and that, however short the career of victory may be, it must always lead beyond the first steps in pursuit.'[43] The aim of advancing towards or even catching up the enemy was to turn its retreat into a rout, to destroy its military capability and thereby bring a peace settlement closer. Only such pursuit could make the battle a decisive battle and enable the campaign or the war to be decided within a few days or weeks. Wars thus became shorter, and their outcome lay essentially in the hands of the military.[44] The age of the war of devastation, sapping the enemy's will by inflicting constant damage on its territory, came to an end. From now on, the concentration of forces in space and time would be the strategic key to success, and battle the decisive factor in war. This kind of warfare, whose great masters were Napoleon Bonaparte on the French side and Helmuth von Moltke on the German side, gave the army an aura of heroism that resulted in its special place within nineteenth- and twentieth-century society.[45] But all this became possible only when highly disciplined troops were available to be deployed in a decisive battle, and when they were able and willing to hunt down and wipe out the defeated enemy.

The construction of a disciplined army well trained in tactics was not, of course, without historical precedents; it could pick up where earlier European tendencies had left off and fall back on much older military traditions. A good example here is the Orange military reform that was reputedly the core for the new discipline; many of its ideas, through transfer from neo-Stoicism and adaptation to changed circumstances, may be considered a revival of Roman military thinking.[46] To be sure, the model was not the citizen levy on which Machiavelli had pinned his hopes,[47] but the professional armies of the late Republic and early Empire, in which military discipline owed more to patriotic motivation than to an ethos of duty. Nevertheless, in the long formative history of tactically well-trained and disciplined foot soldiers, the burgher and peasant contingents of the late Middle Ages played an important role alongside the Roman model; they had managed to hold their own against the superior technology of the feudal knights only by keeping their battle lines in a disciplined manner – and in this their corporations and guilds had often been a decisive element.[48]

From the sixteenth century onward, the process of creating military discipline was able to link up with these and other traditions, and this was an important difference between Europe and parts of the world where semi-nomadic hunters and gatherers determined the shape of war. These latter regions never went beyond the initial stages of the creation of a disciplined army, and sometimes not even that far, since the use of force that is a natural part of daily life for nomadic peoples could pass almost seamlessly into the fighting of war. The distinction between war and peace, which had elsewhere made itself felt in people's lives since the development of agriculture and towns, was less significant in the social organization of nomadic peoples, who lived in something like a permanent state of war. It is certainly no accident that the new wars have spread mainly where there is no long tradition of military discipline, and where forms of violence similar to 'small-war' practices are an established part of the lifestyle. Nor is it necessary to stress that a clear separation did not develop between the use of force and economic activity; the mechanisms limiting violence were based not on discipline but on 'the warrior's honour', and in recent decades these have been broken and destroyed by the ever more invasive presence of automatic weapons and the staple fare of the Western culture industry. The unchaining of violence in the new wars stems not least from a combination of kalashnikov and Hollywood – the simplest Russian weapons technology and the extreme depiction of violence in American feature films.[49]

The symmetry of war after its statization

In the long term, of course, the battlefield concentration of military force in mid-seventeenth-century Europe was successful only because it was part of a general political trend which rewarded individual states for their acceptance of military symmetry and any associated disadvantages; the reward, paid in the currency of the recognition of sovereignty, theoretically placed them on an equal footing with the major European powers. Had states not been so prevented from adopting such asymmetrical strategies as people's war to produce an otherwise unattainable balance with superior enemy forces, the distinctions between deployment zone and battlefield, rear and front, combatants and non-combatants, weapons of war and civilian equipment would have broken down and war would have engulfed the whole population. Until the twentieth century, in fact, this almost never happened. Only the Spanish guerrilla war against Napoleon, and to some extent the Russian partisan war of the autumn and winter of 1812, resorted to this method; perhaps the South Tyrol uprising of 1809 against the Bavarian occupying power could also be mentioned in this context.[50] It is true that Prussian reformers contemplated such ideas between 1807 and 1812, but they never took them beyond the drawing board. Clausewitz, who at least for a time enthusiastically championed people's war and saw it as a means of restoring the morale of Prussia and Germany,[51] briefly summarized the objections then being raised against it:

> It [people's war] has its advocates and its opponents: the latter either considering it in a political sense as a revolutionary means, a state of anarchy declared lawful, which is as dangerous as a foreign enemy to social order at home; or on military grounds, conceiving that the result is not commensurate with the expenditure of the nation's strength.[52]

Clausewitz's analytic account of the principles underlying people's war, as distinct from inter-state war, clearly draws out its asymmetrical nature:

> It follows from the very nature of the thing that defensive means thus widely dispersed, are not suited to great blows requiring concentrated action in time and space. Its operation, like the process of evaporation in physical nature, is according to the surface. The greater that surface and the greater the contact with the enemy's army, consequently the more that army spreads itself out, so much the greater will be the effects of arming the nation. Like a slow gradual heat, it destroys the foundations of the enemy's army.[53]

In the anti-Napoleonic War of Liberation (1813) this asymmetrical warfare was not the dominant form, nor was it during the Franco–Prussian War of 1870–1 when the Republican government in Paris, following the fall of Napoleon III, attempted to make up for the crushing defeats of the regular army by mobilizing the entire nation in accordance with the model of 1793.[54] Despite tendencies in another direction, both wars were ultimately decided on the battlefield.

What took shape in Europe after the Thirty Years' War was a highly robust political system geared to symmetry. Wars were still fought and frontiers were still moved,[55] but forms of warfare threatening to the system were either prevented or kept to peripheral sectors far from its centre. The principle of symmetry underlying this political system proved itself on three levels, and if asymmetries began to appear on any one of these levels, the other two were capable of checking and balancing them or of nipping them in the bud. The three levels in question were those of *military strategy*, *political rationality* and *international legality*. With regard to international legality, symmetrical relations were established through the mutual recognition of sovereignty; this also involved acceptance of the equality of states under international law, which, even if considerable differences persisted on account of population size and geographical area, represented an important means to prevent stronger states from resorting to asymmetrical forms of warfare. Any state that did resort to them placed its equality bonus in jeopardy, with consequences potentially so serious that it was even considered preferable to give up a war as lost and to accept territorial losses.

On the level of political rationality, the most important of the three, structural symmetry, had a stabilizing function: that is, the principle of symmetry made it possible to estimate fairly reliably the relationship of forces between individual states, to compare the size of another country's army and military budget with one's own and to ensure through precautionary alliances that a potential enemy did not attain military supremacy. Since the armed forces within Europe were fundamentally similar to one another, a simple numerical calculation was enough to make the comparison. On various occasions this led to an arms race, but often the result was to stabilize the situation in respect of armament policy, as each side measured the preparedness of its own military forces in relation to the efforts undertaken by the other side. Countries thus armed themselves against a real rather than an imaginary opponent – which had the advantage that a position of superiority or inferiority could easily be established and corrected. This is not possible when a symmetrical opponent is lacking; then one arms against a threat of one's own imagination, not against a real, visible adversary.

In principle, this was the situation that marked or guaranteed the rationality of political actors until the end of the East–West conflict.

German soldiers in trenches, 1914
In the autumn of 1914, fighting on the Western front became frozen into a
war of position. The following years witnessed matériel and attrition battles
on the main sections, in which neither side, despite huge losses, was able to
gain a decisive advantage. Photograph: Ullstein.

It was all dependent, of course, on the maintenance of symmetry –
and on agreement that neither side would respond to temporary partial asymmetry with a strategy involving the creation of systematic
asymmetry. In fact, efforts to balance out temporary asymmetries
had the effect of stabilizing the system as a whole.[56] This may be
illustrated by the Prussian reforms following the defeats of Jena
and Auerstedt, which partly sought to offset the superiority that
the French had gained from changes introduced in the wake of
the Revolution.[57] European politics have followed this principle for
centuries.

It is debatable whether the system built upon symmetries in military strategy, political rationality and international legality first broke down in the First World War or the Second World War, or only with the fall of the Soviet Union and the rise of the United States to sole dominance. The First World War mobilized all the resources of industry and recruited large numbers of civilians for the arms sector, which, if it had not functioned smoothly, would have brought the war machine at the front to a standstill. Workers producing arms became semi-combatants, so that there was no longer such a clear distinction between participants and non-participants in war. The long duration of the war, and the failure of all attempts to force a military resolution, deeply shook faith in the rationality of the old political conditions;[58] the war ushered in a new age in international law, and the right to declare war became limited to cases of defence against attack. This nullified the 'legal equality' of the two belligerents, since the argument of self-defence only applied when one side had violated the ban on a war of aggression.

This trend continued in the Second World War, when the Wehrmacht's war of plunder and annihilation, especially in the East, the partisan war in Russia and the Balkans, and finally the strategic bombing of German cities by the Western Allies effaced the dividing line between combatants and non-combatants that had until then been largely respected. The consequence was total war. Even after 1945 the dividing line could no longer be reliably established: the nuclear stalemate between the two superpowers, the USA and the USSR, ultimately rested upon each side taking hostage of the other's civilian population, with the help of strategic bombers and intercontinental missiles.[59] Even if military strategists and arms planners on both sides found it difficult to accept, there was a clear assumption in policy making that no major war could be fought between the superpowers; that, if one should break out, it would mean the end of human civilization. The only policy dispute was over the level at which the nuclear stalemate should and could be established. The history of 'large war' seemed to be over, and not a few voices added that the history of war itself had come to an end.[60]

When war is no longer worthwhile

Hopes that the end of history would bring the end of war and usher in an era of lasting peace did not first appear in the closing decades of the twentieth century; they go back to the eighteenth century[61] and even – as a utopian or eschatological vision – to the Old Testament, where passages in this spirit can be found in the Book of Isaiah, for example. It was in the age of the Enlightenment that social-economic and political trends finally made an age of peace appear not only desirable but possible, or even probable, and certain observations at the time of the Industrial Revolution also suggested that war would lose its appeal as the agrarian economy became less important.

In his essay *Perpetual Peace* Immanuel Kant drew together the constitutional-republican and social-economic strands as the basis for an expectation that the age of war was ending and an era of peace was dawning. 'For the spirit of commerce sooner or later takes hold of every people, and it cannot exist side by side with war.'[62] More than all the 'motives of morality', the power of money causes states 'to promote the noble cause of peace', and 'wherever in the world there is a threat of war ... they will try to prevent it by mediation'.[63] This approach was taken up and developed by later writers such as Auguste Comte, Herbert Spencer and, more recently, Joseph Schumpeter.[64] Thus, in his critique of the Marxist theory of imperialism (which assumed that a growing tendency to wars of conquest and subjugation would result from the cyclical accumulation crises of capitalism), Schumpeter insisted that 'capitalist wars of conquest', if they happened, would be due not to the capitalist form of society but to the need for prestige evident among non-bourgeois professions and mentalities. Where the laws of capitalism did assert themselves, they would

> tell ... against the use of military force and for peaceful arrangements, even where the balance of pecuniary advantage is clearly on the side of war which, under modern circumstances, is not in general very likely. As a matter of fact, the more completely capitalist the structure and attitude of a nation, the more pacifist – and the more prone to count the costs of war – we observe it to be.[65]

With the development and enforcement of capitalist forms of society on a world scale, war will thus gradually become 'outdated' and – unless this tendency is interrupted by collective regression or blocked by the strengthening of non-capitalist powers – will at some stage totally disappear. According to Schumpeter, then, the spirit of commerce demanded the emergence and dissemination of a post-heroic mentality, which would eventually become dominant in society and marginalize social layers and groups oriented to war and violence.[66]

But how was it possible to assist the political as well as the social breakthrough of a post-heroic mentality resting upon a capitalist vision of the economy? Kant spoke of a republican constitution in which there would be no place for mercenaries or a professional army:

> If, as is inevitably the case under this constitution, the consent of the citizens is required to decide whether or not war is to be declared, it is very natural that they will have great hesitation in embarking on so dangerous an enterprise. For this would mean calling down on themselves all the miseries of war, such as doing the fighting themselves, supplying the costs of the war from their own resources, painfully making good the ensuing devastation and, as the crowning evil, having to take upon themselves a burden of debt which will embitter peace itself and which can never be paid off on account of the constant threat of new wars.[67]

Now, empirical research into the causes of war assumes that Kant's linkage of utilitarian calculation, political participation and a peace orientation does actually correspond to quite a well-verified claim: that democratically governed states do not wage war *against one another*. This does not in principle rule out war against non-democratic states, of course, and the willingness to engage in such war increases when the army consists of professional soldiers rather than conscripts. Solid grounds can certainly be given for the postulate of democratic peace, but it is rather lacking in predictive power. For there are not so many democracies in the world (since the 1940s most of them have been part of the NATO military alliance), and it is by no means clear whether and under what conditions democracies are prepared to wage war against non-democratic states.[68]

In connection with Kant's reflections, a number of researchers on peace and conflict issues have developed the vision of a gradual disappearance of war on a world scale. They too start from the Kantian assumptions: the pacifying effects of a capitalist economic ethos and a high degree of political participation on the part of those who would be affected by the consequences of war.[69] But what this usually overlooks, or underestimates, is the extent to which these two factors are bound up with the international state order. As this has been eroded in recent years, hopes of a gradual disappearance of (now economically unattractive) wars have probably also become more fragile. Inter-state wars, especially when conducted by highly developed industrial nations, are no longer worthwhile; any conceivable return is smaller than the damage that must be factored in.

This balance sheet holds true, of course, only in terms of the country as a whole; it does not apply to the warlords, civil war factions and regional militias who set up on their own account in the new wars. And the balance sheets change even more when it is a question not of symmetrical war but of the costs associated with asymmetrical strategies. For, as we have seen, whereas symmetrical wars tend to result in a symmetrical distribution of costs between the belligerents – so that the incentive to economize by avoiding war is the same for both sides – this is precisely not the case in asymmetrical wars.

4

THE ECONOMICS OF FORCE IN THE NEW WARS

War on the cheap

The ever-rising costs of new weapons systems, as well as party-political disputes on how to fund them, have created the impression that war – or a defensive capability – becomes more expensive in parallel with the advances of technology, and that only a handful of rich countries can now afford to have an army in full working order. In a sense this is not a wrong impression, for the costs of purchasing and maintaining nearly all weapons systems – from battle tanks to fighter aircraft, not to speak of satellite reconnaissance or missile defence – have increased several times over the last few decades. This inevitably led to a situation where the arsenals of regular armies were always running short. Apart from the issue of whether it makes sense militarily, no state today is able to field as extensive an array of armoured units, air fleets and naval forces as it deployed during the Second World War. Crammed with electronics, the military machine has simply become too costly.

On the other hand, the new wars are downright cheap – or, at least, it is cheap to prepare and wage them. For they are generally fought with light weapons (automatic rifles, landmines, multiple rocket launchers) and use the civilian infrastructure in such a way that pick-ups take the place of jeeps, light trucks and armoured personnel carriers. Where the occasional heavy weapon is deployed, it is usually an item left behind by one of the powers in the East–West conflict, something that otherwise would have no more than scrap value. There is scarcely any demand for heavy weapons, because the

Soldiers in Sierra Leone, 2000
The new wars are fought mainly with light weapons and civilian transport.
Automatic rifles, landmines and pick-ups form the logistical and operational backbone of militia forces, providing them with reconnaissance vehi-
cles, troop carriers and fast-moving combat transport. Photograph: Reuters.

new wars are not waged against a similarly armed enemy but mainly
employ long-term violence against large parts of the civilian population. For the characteristic combination of massacre and ambush,
light weapons and unarmoured means of transport are perfectly ad-
equate. And since the flooding of the market, especially with Russian
products, has often driven the price of automatic weapons below the
cost of production, not much money is required to arm the followers
of militia leaders and warlords, rebels and revolutionaries, and to
turn them into a much-feared army within a short space of time.[1]
Finally, it costs even less to deploy these troops than to recruit and
arm them, for they can take care of themselves through extortion,
plunder and robbery, in accordance with the principle that war has
to sustain war.

Thus, whereas it is true that the military of the OECD world is
becoming ever costlier to run, the militias and warlord forces that
actually wage the new wars are considerably cheaper than the regular armies of earlier decades. Most likely, this is what makes the

new wars so threatening and widens the circle of those able to fight them. In the end, of course, they will probably prove costlier to society than regular inter-state wars used to be, since they eventually cause greater devastation over a wide area and have more profound long-term consequences for society as a whole. Nearly all wars are fought at the expense of the future: in inter-state wars this takes the form of debts that have to be paid by future generations; in the new wars, the very possibility of a peaceful life is ruined for a long time to come.

As we have seen, the statization of war in Europe was accompanied with major changes in the conduct of war. The costs continually spiralled upwards – both for the training of professional soldiers and for the more widespread purchase of heavy weapons – so that soon they could be borne only by a powerful economy in association with an ever more efficient state apparatus. By contrast, the trends converging in the new wars went in the opposite direction, towards military indiscipline and lack of professionalism.[2] This became especially apparent with regard to the recruitment of children and young people, who required little training in the use of today's quick-firing guns. The significance of heavy weapons declined, and the absorption of the social surplus product, instead of being legally regulated by a state system of taxes, took place arbitrarily and excessively through extortion, plunder and robbery. These three factors – predominance of light weapons, ability to use almost untrained fighters, funding of war through robbery or trade in illegal goods – were the main reasons why the statization of war broke down and the privatization of military force once again became economically attractive. Finally, we should not fail to mention that, from the fifteenth to the sixteenth century onward, war and preparations for war in Europe always gave an impetus to technological development and economic modernization as well as resulting in additional burdens and devastation, but that the new wars have nothing but destructive effects. They leave behind ravaged landscapes, maimed generations and social anomie – certainly not the kind of prospects needed to build a peacetime economy. Such disastrous long-term outcomes are the reverse side of the fact that the short-term costs are rather small.[3]

Comparison with the social-economic effects of war in early modern Europe shows that the new wars can hardly be said to have a state-building function.[4] Rather, they should be seen as wars involving the sheer collapse of states and the destruction of societies, with no prospects for a sustainable future. After such a war the societies in question not only have to rely on imports of food and medicine;

they also require state support, at least to reconvert the social relations of exchange to an economy in which people are oriented more to the dividends of peace than to those of war. The new wars also generate neocolonial structures, since they destroy for a long time the capacities for self-organization and make it impossible for society to make its own decisions about the path of development to be followed. In these conditions, societies that have access to aid, a functioning social-political order and elite elements resistant to corruption (for example, within the framework of a UN protectorate) enjoy distinct advantages in comparison with other societies that collapse unnoticed and in whose future destiny scarcely anyone takes an interest.

The most important reason why the new wars are so cheap, and therefore so easy to start, is that they are funded through asymmetrical relations of exchange imposed upon society. The money for classical inter-state wars was skimmed off the social surplus product, and this had no direct effects on exchange relations within society, except for supply bottlenecks and the resulting formation of prices. It is true that informal and partly criminal economies came into being, but they were more a feature of the immediate postwar period than of the war itself, and black markets soon disappeared as the supply of goods increased and currencies stabilized. In the new wars, by contrast, force becomes the dominant element in exchange relations themselves – either by being bought in order to produce certain results, or because the exchange of equivalents is overlaid or completely replaced with extortion and open threats of violence. Whereas classical inter-state wars are no longer worthwhile, because they cost more than they yield for each of the participants, the new wars are highly lucrative for many of the participants, because in the short term the force used in them yields more than it costs – and the long-term costs are borne by others.

The cheapness of the new wars is not only due to their being fought with light weapons; it also has to do with the availability of young people who want to attach themselves to a warlord or militia leader in return for a kind of livelihood and the prospect of an otherwise unattainable social reputation. Their decision is all the easier since their weapons will help them secure what they need for survival. With reference to the intra-state wars in West Africa, Peter Lock pointedly writes:

> For young men 'being a soldier' is the best means of social participation, and besides it is likely that their chances of survival in today's Sierra Leone are incomparably greater than in the chaos of 'civil

society' paralysed by war. The role of a so-called child soldier is not only seductive for rootless children; it is also a 'rational choice', to put it in the jargon of an economistic viewpoint.[5]

These youngsters are a permanent source of recruitment for the war entrepreneurs – whether they are simply picked up off the street, armed and deployed for a while, as in the wars of sub-Saharan Africa, or whether they are put through a process of ideological preparation and armament, as in the Koranic schools of the Taliban in Afghanistan, before being sent off to fight. 'All the warlords had used boy soldiers', writes Ahmed Rashid about the Afghan wars of the 1980s, 'some as young as 12 years old, and many were orphans with no hope of having a family, an education or a job except soldiering. The Taliban with their linkages to the Pakistani *madrasas* [Koranic schools] encouraged thousands of children to enlist and fight. Entire units were made up of kids as loaders for artillery batteries, and ammunition carriers, for guarding installations and as fighters.'[6] In short, children and young people are a central part of the new wars and contribute decisively to their low cost.

No expensive state apparatus of registration and coercion is required to channel these youngsters into war en masse.[7] Their exclusion from regular economic activity, their hunger and their lack of peacetime social prospects automatically drive them into the arms of the warring parties. Under these conditions, war represents not only an opportunity to secure their physical survival, but also a way of achieving social recognition that would never be accorded them if they did not have a gun in their hand. One of their major concerns might be either to gain rapid access to the status symbols of the Western culture industry, or to combat the triumphal march of those same consumption goods, as most of the jihad ideologies teach. Both of these seemingly contradictory motives share the promise of prestige and recognition. It is therefore not enough to view the armed youth of the new wars purely in terms of the struggle for scarce material resources, especially water and food; the social resource of recognition nearly always carries just as much weight, if not more:

> With gun in hand, a young man feels for the first time in his life that he is respected by others, even if it is merely fear that he perceives as respect. Force in the shape of an automatic weapon becomes the means of defending himself against social exclusion. Force promises access to the world of industrial mass consumption, which is constantly present in the media even in remote corners of the earth.[8]

The experience of humiliation, together with a sudden power that has never been subject to military discipline, leads to excesses of violence in which pent-up hatred explodes in wild fantasies of omnipotence. 'These people without arms or legs', writes Peter Scholl-Latour of war invalids in Sierra Leone,

> are victims of the boy soldiers of the 'United Revolutionary Front' (RUF), or the especially feared 'West Side Boys' who, high on drugs or alcohol, get their kicks from hacking limbs off civilians completely uninvolved in the war. In Freetown, there are said to have been 8,000 such cases of arbitrary maiming. In the last phase of this horror story, it must have been great fun drawing lots to decide which part of the body to cut off, from which person and whether with a machete or a hatchet.[9]

Before writing this off as an African peculiarity, one should compare it with reports of what happened when Taliban forces, who were said to have a certain religiously grounded discipline, captured the Afghan city of Mazar-i Sharif:

> A Taliban commander later said that Mullah Omar had given them permission to kill for two hours, but they had killed for two days. The Taliban went on a killing frenzy, driving their pick-ups up and down the narrow streets of Mazar to the left and right and killing everything that moved – shop owners, cart pullers, women and children, shoppers and even goats and donkeys. Contrary to all injunctions of Islam, which demands immediate burial, bodies were left to rot on the streets.[10]

In such massacres, ethnic differences are repeatedly used to justify the excesses; but although they intensify the violence, they do not cause it. The real cause is the gun-fed rise of socially excluded layers, who take revenge for past humiliations by killing those with a regular livelihood or perhaps even a modest prosperity. As they have never known a working life and therefore have no idea of the toil associated with it, they often view the structures of civil society as something to be pillaged and destroyed as the fancy takes them. That this is not limited to the so-called Third World may be seen from the wars that accompanied the break-up of Yugoslavia, especially the war in Bosnia. 'One of the earliest, deepest, and most pervasive effects of the fighting had been to turn the social pyramid on its head,' David Rieff reported:

> The bourgeoisie had been ruined and demoralized by the war. With every passing month its material situation worsened. For those who had had little before the fighting started, the situation was reversed. Simple boys from the countryside and tough kids from the towns found that their guns made them the ones who could start amassing Deutschmarks and the privileges, sexual and otherwise. It often really was a question of the first being last and the last first. Whether it was in Sarajevo, or Tuzla, or Mostar, young men dressed in Rambo-like gear could be found lounging in the cafés, or be seen driving their girls around in the few civilian vehicles left in any particular area.[11]

Rieff also points out that, on both the Serbian and the Bosnian side, it was the big-city underworld ranging from street hoodlums to mafia gangs who occupied the key positions in the so-called paramilitary groups.[12]

The entrepreneurs of the new wars have not drawn only on socially excluded young people, but these are by far the largest and most easily activated group of potential recruits. Young people also display a remarkable insouciance in the face of danger: fear of death rarely touches their thoughts and actions, and their instinct for self-preservation, especially in puberty, is considerably less marked than among adults. But this also means that they have fewer inhibitions in using violence, make no allowances for defenceless people and tend to be especially cruel and brutal – characteristics that make them the most feared participants in the new wars.[13] Warlords tend to rely on child soldiers when they are faced with UN peacekeeping troops; this regularly causes great distress to the blue helmets, who hesitate to open fire and even prefer to surrender rather than become involved in fighting. They may then acquire considerable value as hostages in the negotiations through which the warlords seek to consolidate their power. If these are successful, the resources 'invested' in the war will have proved worthwhile, since international recognition will enable the regime built on robbery and violence to stabilize itself through international recognition.

Often, however, either warlords end up quarrelling with other entrepreneurs of war or some of their junior leaders, believing they have not had their fare share of the booty, start new wars to get their hands on the big pot of power and riches. Although it is not totally excluded that warlordism will transmute into a proto-state form of rule, and that a reasonably stable state will emerge after a certain time, a breakdown is much more likely to occur, mostly because too many individuals around the warlord follow his model by striking out on their own along the paths he has already beaten.[14]

The bonding charisma of the warlord or guerrilla leader disappears as the hostilities die out, and the disappointments associated with the peace process then create supporters for those who advocate a continuation of war. They are joined by all who once flocked to a warlord in search of prestige and recognition, and who are mistrustful of peace because they fear it will confront them with just as many problems as before the war. In their eyes, peace cannot fulfil what the war promised to deliver. Therefore, farsighted warlords do not seriously tackle the dangerous project of peacefully consolidating their rule, and those who do take it up usually fall victim to a rebellion by younger elements. Precisely because war is so cheap, the costs of peace are so high.

Sexual violence in the strategy and economics of the new wars

Since time immemorial, the violence of war has always been directed against women as well as men. 'They killed the men and led the women and children into slavery' – such is the image presented by ancient historians when they report the capture of a city and the fate of its inhabitants. Whereas the men are treated as enemies to be overcome, the women and (especially female) children are part of the booty that naturally falls to the conquerors. Homer's account of the struggle for Troy and its eventual capture already revolves around the theme of woman as treasure of war: it was because of Helen that the war began in the first place; Briseis becomes an object in the dispute between Agamemnon and Achilles, so that the son of Peleus refuses to fight and the war keeps dragging on; and in the end the women rescued from the flames of Troy are shared out among the victors. Part of the booty, a prize of victory, a sex object for soldiers: armed struggle has never been an affair only between men.

The strong form of this generalization, however, which presents violence against women as an ever identical phenomenon, an anthropological constant,[15] overlooks the extent to which it has varied historically in both scale and intensity. Evidently there was always violence against women in the classical inter-state wars, but since the eighteenth century at the latest it has been considered a war crime for which the penalty has usually been death. Concern for military discipline and fear of the spread of sexually transmitted diseases[16] has often played more of a role here than respect for and enforcement of human rights, with the result that mass rapes have no longer been a semi-institutional part of war and any individual cases have been severely punished.

The Geneva Convention relative to the Protection of Civilian Persons in Time of War (1949) requires belligerents, in both inter-state and intra-state wars, to treat with humanity all persons who take no part in the fighting or who have already laid down their weapons, and to ensure that they are 'protected especially against all acts of violence or threats thereof and against insults and pub-lic curiosity. Women shall be especially protected against any attack on their honour, in particular against rape, enforced prostitution, or any form of indecent assault.'[17] It also explicitly holds the belliger-ents responsible for the protection of non-combatants: 'The Party to the conflict in whose hands protected persons may be is responsible for the treatment accorded to them by its agents, irrespective of any individual responsibility which may be incurred.'[18]

Why have the new wars of the last two decades shown little or no respect for these and similar provisions, which did largely suc-ceed in preventing wartime violence against women and children? In fact, one cannot help but think that sexual violence has become an especially effective instrument of the new wars. 'Rapes allow you to save on bombs,' observed one woman in Zagreb during the break-up of Yugoslavia. 'With rapes you can achieve ethnic cleansing more ef-fectively, and at lesser cost. Rape is a war economy.'[19] If this is true – and much suggests that it is, in wars whose aim is to expel large sections of the population – women are no longer just booty, tro-phies or sex objects; they have become the conqueror's main target of attack. Thus, along with the destruction of cultural possessions[20] and the massacre of sections of the male population, the mass rapes and rape camps in Bosnia or East Timor[21] are the third element of a political-military strategy based on large-scale 'ethnic cleansing'.

Such a strategy is not necessarily new. It appeared in a series of wars in the early twentieth century (in the First World War, for ex-ample, when Armenians were expelled en masse from the Ottoman Empire, or in the aftermath of the Greek–Turkish war of 1922, when large population groups were forcibly resettled in the Balkans and Asia Minor[22]); and it was used in Nazi planning for the war of ex-termination in the East,[23] as well as in the expulsion of the German population from their home areas in the Balkans and the former eastern territories of the Reich. These population transfers may be regarded as a policy success, in so far as they laid the foundation for a redrawing of state frontiers or a reconfiguration of multina-tional empires into a number of nation states. After the end of the East–West conflict, when frozen borders began to melt and to shift, the idea again occurred of employing the instrument of 'ethnic cleansing'. In the existing conditions of world politics and intensive media coverage, however, it was clear that a policy of openly violent 'ethnic cleansing' or genocide would provoke fierce reactions on the part of neighbouring states, and that it would be difficult to achieve international recognition of the anticipated 'gains'.

The strategy of sexual violence – ranging from mass rape to the internment and systematic violation of selected women and ending in their deportation or in public displays of pregnancy[24] – may be thought of as a policy of 'ethnic cleansing' in the grand style, without genocide. It makes a system out of fear and trembling, violence and demoralization, and forces most of a population to give up their homes and belongings 'voluntarily' and to leave the land of their birth with no more than a couple of suitcases. The three main stages in this strategy of fear are the execution of leading figures in political and cultural life as well as of potential resistance fighters; the burning or blowing up of sacred buildings and cultural monuments;[25] and the systematic rape and forced pregnancy of women in the section of the population targeted for expulsion.[26]

This puts in concrete form what was described above as the re-placement of battle with massacre.[27] The use of violence against en-emy civilians in the new wars – so that the concentration of force in the battlefield is replaced with the diffusion of force across entire landscapes – is here not so much (or perhaps not at all) the result of indiscipline among armed contingents as the outcome of calculated planning. And, if violence against women becomes more significant than violence against men, this is because it is actually one of the aims of the war, not because aggressive male behaviour is an anthropo-logical constant or a peculiarity of a particular civilization. In the classical inter-state wars, which were decided by battles and great circling manoeuvres, sexual violence on enemy territory was dys-functional: it slowed down the movement of troops, increased the danger of infection with sexually transmitted diseases and generally undermined morale. The provisions of international law for the pro-tection of civilians fitted in well with the organizational rationality of the military apparatus, and they were therefore enforced with the necessary vigour. In the new wars, on the other hand, which in this respect look like a throwback to late-medieval forms of warfare,[28] rape is often highly functional: it saps people's will to hold out, despite adverse, life-threatening circumstances, until better times arrive in the land of their birth. Since the local political-military leadership does not prevent or punish sexual violence against women, but actually orders and organizes it, armed intervention

Francisco de Goya, *Desastres de la Guerra* **N. 30**
In partisan warfare the dividing line between combatants and non-combatants is eroded. Women, in particular, increasingly become the object of every conceivable kind of violence and cruelty, as Francisco de Goya already depicted in his cycle 'Desastres de la guerra' in 1810–1815. Photograph: Corbis.

by an outside force becomes the only way of enforcing international law.

Whereas in battle the uniformed male body is the object of attack, a massacre is mainly directed at the female body – whether through rape or in orgies of violence whose evident purpose is to remove any resemblance between the corpse (which may also be male) and a human being. The military function of battlefield violence against a uniformed body is easy to understand, since the soldier who is its target is both instrument and representative of a political will that has to be broken by force of arms.[29] The means of enforcing and asserting that will are taken away through an act that constitutes a physical and moral blow to the enemy. Is the same true of the asymmetrical violence against women and girls that is supposed to help drive certain sections of the population from the land of their birth?

Some feminist authors have suggested that sexual violence against women should be seen as a form of communication between men. 'Rape by a conquering soldier', writes Susan Brownmiller, 'destroys all remaining illusions of power and property for men of the defeated side. The body of a raped woman becomes a ceremonial battlefield, a parade ground for the victor's trooping of the colours.'[30] This explains why in the new wars – as also in the Thirty Years' War – many rapes take place in public places, or at least in the presence of the husband, father and other relatives of the victim. Their quasi-military significance consists in the demonstrative humiliation and emasculation of the enemy, who has it literally brought home to him that he cannot protect 'his' women and that it is therefore time to take them and himself away from the disputed territory forever.[31] Here, too, the attack is directed against the enemy's will, but it takes place through the violence inflicted on the woman's body. The shaming of the body destroys it as a symbol of wholeness and inviolability, so that the enemy will give up the self-assertive will to fight. In a sense, therefore, the attack no longer strikes at the organs of state power – that is possible only symmetrically, with similarly armed organs of another state power – but targets the ethnic-cultural identity represented by the woman and the community's power to reproduce itself which she ensures.

As a political-military strategy, mass rape in wartime has found its way into societies where – at least according to official figures – the violation of women used to be a very rare occurrence.[32] Islamic societies in particular belonged to this category. But the rape of at least 200,000 women in Bangladesh by (Muslim) Pakistani soldiers before and during the war of 1971, as well as the previously mentioned rape of Hazara women in and around Mazar-i Sharif by Taliban forces,[33] shows that violence as a calculated part of military strategy is independent of traditional patterns of behaviour. In this connection, mention should also be made of the armed groups affiliated to the Islamic Salvation Front (FIS) in Algeria, who kidnap girls and young women from Berber villages and keep raping them until they become pregnant.[34] The point of this is not so much to provide sex slaves for the leaders of these groups as to destroy the Berber communities by wounding their self-esteem and ensuring that the women, pregnant in a still traditional social order, no longer appear as potential wives and mothers. The Serbian Chetniks in Bosnia or the Indonesian army in East Timor pursued the same objective: to smash up a social community, to shatter family ties and to interrupt the sequence of generations, thereby breaking its members' will to assert their identity. The rape strategies apparent in a number of the new wars are thus a continuation of war by other means.

But it is not always the case in the new wars that rape is part of a strategy planned by the political-military leadership. The rapes accompanying the genocide in Rwanda, which probably affected hundreds of thousands of women,[35] as well as the practice of rape in West Africa's civil wars, in Chad, in Congo and in Indonesia,[36] should be decoded more in terms of an economy than a strategy of violence. That which, in a quasi-military strategy, is subordinate to the functional dimension is here the prime consideration: the rape of women as a prize for victors and conquerors. Nevertheless, these are not one-off actions limited to a short period of time after the end of hostilities; rather, they testify to the extensive sexualization of violence that is observable in nearly all the new wars. The use of force, which has become automatic with the development and introduction of remote weapons (and especially the transition to firearms), is here once more in thrall to the libido. It is no longer an assault on the enemy's corporeality that is meant to break his will and determination, but rather an infliction of suffering and torment that is evidently experienced as pleasurable, and at the end of which death often lies. It would seem from various first-hand reports, however, that death is the unintended outcome rather than the deliberate aim of the agonizing wound. War here becomes one big torture machine whose purpose is to produce pain and suffering but not to enforce a political will.[37]

> The militia in Mexico liked the machete ... the Serbian and Algerian slaughterers favoured hatchets, axes, sawn-off shotguns, iron bars, daggers and butchers' knives. These are the tools of bloody hand-to-hand fighting. The aim of the massacre is not to eliminate victims without trace but to mutilate the body. The victims are slaughtered like cattle, their bodies hacked to resemble pieces of meat, their sexual organs cut away. In so far as there is any religious feeling behind the practice of massacre, it is not some 'fundamentalist' idea of God, but reversion to the bloody and archaic ritual of human sacrifice, a sacrifice made by the murderous group to its idol, which is itself.[38]

This is not the least of the reasons why a number of authors have recently analysed rape as a phenomenon in the realm of torture, not of sexuality.[39] The similarities are here especially great with the wars of the sixteenth and seventeenth centuries, when sexual violence and pleasure in the infliction of pain (not only on men) also belonged to the economy of war. Sexual sadism, writes David Rieff, is part of every 'ethnic cleansing'.[40] This is true, but sexual sadism has evidently not needed a strategic directive for 'ethnic cleansing' to become a widespread feature of the new wars.[41] Peter Lock has pointed out that, in the process of economic modernization, men have lost the special role they had in traditional societies, but that at the same time the tough, self-assertive fighting man has been held up as a masculine ideal in American films shown all around the world. 'For want of cultural-emancipatory and economic alternatives, male identity is itself constructed through acts of violence that convey a sense of easy superiority. Men's lost position in the production process is replaced with participation in the social production of violence.'[42] Since in societies with more than 50 per cent youth unemployment, it is chiefly male teenagers and young men who have to endure social marginalization day in, day out in peacetime conditions, the readiness to taste power (and to make up for everyday humiliation) by employing extreme violence against women is hardly likely to fall away. The warlords and militia leaders are ready to lend a hand in organizing such compensatory experiences.

Refugee flows and humanitarian aid

It is a characteristic of the new wars that they rapidly generate large refugee flows that eventually debouch into various camps on the fringes of the war zone. There, international aid agencies quickly take action to bring in food and medical supplies and try to prevent the outbreak of epidemics. These refugee camps are usually part of the war economy and have considerable significance for the belligerents, who use them as a source of food and medicine. The aid agencies of the United Nations, as well as the humanitarian nongovernmental organizations (NGOs), have thus willy-nilly become a fixed part of the civil war economies, and when they do not intervene on their own initiative they are drawn in with the help of television. As soon as a war and its associated refugees reach a certain threshold of media attention and supply enough pictures for the news programmes in the OECD countries, an almost automatic mechanism is set in train which starts up the flow of international aid. The numbers of donation accounts are ritually blended in with the news, as reporters speak with concern of hunger and poverty or a looming humanitarian disaster. Pictures are shown of famished columns, emaciated old people, begging women and crying children, shortly followed by reports about the aid machine that is already moving into action and flying the first relief supplies into the camps.[43]

What the rich countries mostly regard as positive, charitable action often has disastrous consequences in the war and crisis zones, because the warring parties themselves feed off it. Indeed, the strategists of these wars now include international aid as a logistical element in their operational planning. This is a further factor pushing down the cost of wars; they can be waged all the more easily the less each side has to worry about where its supplies will come from. On bridges, mountain passes or wherever the terrain is suited to roadblocks, armed men stop and search aid convoys and appropriate anything they can use; they let through only what they do not need. The Bosnian Serbs laying siege to Sarajevo, for example, did not allow UN convoys to proceed into the city until they had taken a large part of the relief supplies for themselves.[44] In this way, the UN supported both the besiegers and the besieged, and the international community funded the evil at source while trying to hold it in check. At the very least, humanitarian aid generally becomes something extra that can be used to pay for the continuation of the war; especially if the war is a way for them to make a living, the warring parties cannot then be persuaded to conclude and respect a peace agreement. On the contrary: warlords have learned how, with the help of camera crews, they can start up and control aid deliveries, and they use this as an economical resource for the further pursuit of their wars.[45]

Apart from diverting some of the supplies, warlords profit in other ways from the relief sent in by international agencies. Smaller NGOs, in particular, have to rely on locally available transport to take their aid from ports or runways to the refugee camps, and usually it is only the warlords who have the necessary lorries and pick-ups. Most of all, however, aid workers need protection against all kinds of attacks, and that too is something which only the militia leaders and warlords can provide:

> All aid is interference in the existing conditions; there is no neutral aid. The gangs with the weapons, the warlords and their militias knew that. In Somalia they took control of the aid and the unprotected aid workers. Every delivery of beans, protein cakes or vitamin preparations strengthened their position; every new shipment filled their war chests. For they 'rented out' the lorries and made their 'protection troops' available at a price. Not only did hunger become a weapon in the struggle for power; international aid became an involuntary funder of the brutal gangs fighting the civil war. Terror lived from aid.[46]

There is yet another way in which the militias and warlords are able to use international aid for their own purposes. Every now and then an entire aid shipment 'goes missing' and its contents reappear in small packets at local markets; in this way, warlords keep 'friendly' – and useful – dealers and smugglers in business by giving them doses of international aid and at the same time serve their own economic interests. Those who go under are local producers whose output – if not completely eliminated by the war – suddenly becomes unsaleable and lies around to rot. This collapse of local production structures creates long-term dependence on international aid, with the result that the peacetime economy changes over to the conditions of a war economy. Local farmers and tradesmen, who lived from their own labour until the influx of refugees led to the appearance of camps and the launching of aid programmes, are now dependent upon warlord-controlled economic structures and can survive only by seeking work as lorry drivers, smugglers, dealers – or soldiers.

Refugee flows, and the camps set up to contain them, prove on closer examination to be the web along which an initially local war spreads out into the surrounding region and achieves organizational implantation. By these means an intra-state war can rapidly cross frontiers and develop into a transnational war, and such flows are a major reason for the regular failure of neighbouring states or international agencies to limit and contain the spread of wars. Not only do refugee camps severely damage the often fragile governmental and economic structures of neighbouring countries; aid and support networks soon spring up in these camps for one or another of the warring parties and, to a significant degree, provide it with the means to sustain itself politically and militarily. This in turn makes the camps a target for the other side, as we have seen in the Turkish state's war on underground Kurdish organizations,[47] the Israeli operations in Lebanon, the West Bank and the Gaza Strip,[48] the wars in West Africa, the frontier conflicts between Somalia and Ethiopia, and the civil wars in Chad or Sudan and, most especially, Congo or Angola. In each case, attacks on refugee camps contribute to a further transnationalization of the new wars and make it more difficult to contain or end them.

A mechanism may be seen at work which is analogous to a system of communicating vessels. The more effective a military attack is on a refugee camp, the more negative are the political consequences for the attacker. And, although the victim of the attack suffers organizational or military losses, he wins additional political legitimacy in the eyes of world opinion; as soon as he manages to convert this gain into support from neighbouring countries and international organizations, he is usually able to make good the losses. This is one more reason why the new wars only very rarely have a military resolution and can keep simmering on indefinitely.

The cameras of the world's press and television are an indispensable part of this system, making it possible for military defeats to be converted into political legitimacy gains. It is no accident that almost everywhere belligerents have come to regard these cameras as especially effective weapons; some do all they can to keep journalists away from certain zones of operation, others make every effort to bring them there to record and broadcast events. The media no longer serve a war-reporting function: they have involuntarily become a participant in war, as a direct result of the asymmetrical structure that makes the new wars a confrontation between soldiers and civilians, not between soldiers and soldiers. Media-generated world opinion is thus a resource of war, behind which and in which the combatants on the weaker side seek cover and protection. The political-military importance of the cameras increases in proportion to the asymmetrization of armed conflicts. The traditional neutrality of war reporting was evidently bound up with the symmetry of war, whereas the growth of asymmetrical David-and-Goliath patterns has led to forms of observation that involve taking sides and lending support. The obvious thing for war planners to do, therefore, is to stage themselves in the role of David.[49] The presentation of refugees, crying women and desperately resisting children is the surest means to that end.

When war becomes worthwhile again: economics of the new wars

For a long time, political commentators attached considerably greater significance to the ideological, ethnic and religious dimensions of the new wars than to their economic roots. Of course, those other dimensions are by no means insignificant, but the way in which they are usually overdrawn means that the economic motives of the warring parties tend to be obscured from view. The need for a certain romanticization of the landscapes of violence seems to have greatly contributed to this overemphasis. For, so long as political ideals could be attributed to guerrillas and putschist generals, militias and underground organizations, it was possible to think of wars as liberation struggles in which the aspect of revolutionary progress outweighed the military violence; a focus on the ideological façades that nearly all sides constructed in these wars satisfied the need for clarity and transparency. Self-positioning on either side of the East–West conflict not only gave states the support and protection of larger powers, but also guaranteed that a general view was retained in both camps. It is true that the frontlines repeatedly shifted in spectacular fashion, but in principle it was clear that if one side in a local war tended towards the West, the other turned to the East – and vice versa.

With the end of the East–West conflict, the old ideological references were quickly replaced by ethnic or religious-cultural lines of divide that were supposed to provide once more the necessary orientation and perspective. In fact, these were given so much attention that economic aspects and motives at least equally important for the new wars were overlooked. Even allusions to poverty and social injustice in the war-torn lands are usually of an ideological character, for in the end they offer an explanation of the new wars that does not embrace the action logic of those involved in them but remains stuck at the general, undifferentiated level of socio-economic constellations.

The main reason for the explanatory appeal of ethnic and religious factors is probably that they are capable, at least implicitly, of identifying the new wars as irrational. If it can be shown that these factors are driven by antiquated, unenlightened attitudes and motives, then the obvious course is to tackle them with the instruments of the Enlightenment; the overcoming of irrationalism, and the gradual shifting of behaviour from passions to interests, from traditional ties to individual purposive rationality, should help a peace orientation to gain general acceptance. So long as the economic structures underlying these wars have not been addressed, one can persist in the comfortable belief that rationalization and pacification would go hand in hand – as they do in the OECD countries. On closer examination, however, it becomes apparent that the new wars are in many respects the result of economically purposive rationality, or that people pursuing economic objectives play a major role in them as entrepreneurs, politicians and, not least, fighting men.[50] The figure of the warlord, central in most new wars, may be defined precisely as a combination of entrepreneurial, political and military logic in a single person.[51]

Along with the heightened presence of mercenary firms, the return of the warlord is a reliable indicator that war is once more worthwhile – at least when it can be waged with light weapons and cheap fighters, and when there is scope for linking up with global big business. Without the profitability of force there can be no privatization of war. It is also, indeed especially, true of war that its players take great pains to cream off profits for themselves and to pass on losses to the general public. As we have seen, the rising cost of war in early modern Europe ensured that no private profit could be made directly out of warfare, and an increasingly robust state prevented private entrepreneurs from falling back on the more lucrative military sectors; they could make a return on troop supplies and equipment, but not on the actual conduct of war. The new warlords, on the other hand, again derive their income directly from the fighting of wars, and thereby profit from the collapse of many states that can no longer maintain, or in any way enforce, their monopoly on violence. Disintegration of the state again gives them free rein to privatize and forcibly appropriate the profits of war, while the devastating long-term consequences of the violence have to be borne by society, or what is left of it.

For the warlords, war has become an economically attractive proposition because they can control the distribution of its costs, the privatization of its profits and the socialization of the losses that it entails. Apart from the rules of the global economy, there is no framework to which they must adhere. The economic rationality of their action consists in the fact that they make violence a means to an income, or that through violence they are able to influence exchange relations to their advantage. Warlords and militia leaders exploit the present at the expense of the future, and their preferred means of doing this, in areas under their control, is to shift the basis of the social order away from the exchange of equivalents towards violent appropriation. This should not be confused with plain anarchy in economic life, but should be seen in terms of an imposition of asymmetrical exchange relations. Equivalent exchange rests upon a symmetrical relationship in which two parties with equal rights agree on the value and price of the goods or services to be exchanged. If force is introduced into the relationship, it becomes asymmetrical and the two parties can no longer be considered equal; one uses the threat of violence to define the exchange relationship in a way favourable to himself. This may be described as a privatization of the state's regulatory and protective function, but actually warlordism involves more than that: it imposes fundamental asymmetries on the social relations of exchange. Only thus do the new wars become a worthwhile business.

We should not think of the warlords and militia leaders, putschist generals and charismatic revolutionaries as if they were rationally calculating businessmen who compare various profit forecasts and decide to invest their capital in military force instead of a unit trust. This may be the case with a West European or North American investor who, instead of putting his money in real estate or IT shares, funds a firm of mercenaries with a high reputation in the security sector. In warlord configurations or revolutionary organizations, however, political, ideological, ethnic and religious-cultural considerations also play an important role in making the freedom of entrepreneurial decision a fictitious assumption. Economic analysis of the new wars seeks more to establish their conditions of possibility than to uncover the original motives of those who take part in them. In many cases, however, it shows that political conflicts which may at first have been the main focus become increasingly overlaid with economic interests as the war progresses.[52] The longer the war lasts, the more the economics of violence appears to determine the actions of its main players, and the more the original motives are converted into resources for a war that has taken on an independent dynamic.

The Afghan wars of 1979–2002 clearly illustrate this autonomization of the war economy from the initially political causes of conflict, and also demonstrate how the degree of autonomy correlates with the progressive disintegration of the state. During the Mujahedin war against Afghan government troops and the Soviet army, supply structures covering a small area were highly efficient for guerrilla units operating independently of one another; a technologically superior enemy was given few surfaces to attack, and resources flowing in from Islamic countries and the United States could be deployed with great effect. (According to relatively reliable estimates, the Soviet Union invested some 45 billion dollars in the war in Afghanistan, while the United States and Islamic countries expended roughly 10 billion dollars.) After the Soviet military withdrawal, however, this effectiveness completely turned round into political chaos, since none of the so-called field commanders wanted to transfer their new powers and the associated supply structures to a (still to be constructed) central administration. In fact, central government never had much power in Afghanistan: it always had to rely on support from tribal leaders. But it did create a minimum framework of state regulation, and although never enjoying a European-style monopoly on violence, it kept tribal conflicts sufficiently within bounds for them not to grow into intra-state wars. Precisely this was no longer the case, however. Field commanders turned into warlords, no longer accepted guidelines or instructions and established their own volatile systems of rule which, though occasionally shifting as a result of an offensive or a withdrawal, proved to have astonishing continuity over a period of many years.

No doubt these were essentially kleptocratic economies, which could not develop much more than a perspective of immediate survival and further disinvestment along lines familiar from the war with the Soviet Union.[53] The irrigation system developed over decades was destroyed, large parts of the country were mined and young men who had grown used to the freelance business of war had no inclination to take up hard work again in an unproductive agriculture. In any case, there was not enough to sustain a *closed war economy* operating on the basis of subsistence agriculture, and after the Soviet withdrawal Western and Islamic subsidies threatened to run slowly dry. A gradual transition to an *open war economy* therefore took place. The key feature of this was the growing production of raw opium, which could yield considerable profits on the trade routes to the eastern Mediterranean.[54] The trade in illegal goods thus enabled Afghan warlordism to gain access to global markets, even if this took place by the back door.

Being illegal, the goods required heavy protection for their journey to distant markets, especially where this led across contested territory. The armed followers of warlords found employment in line with their talents and inclinations, and local warlords entered into cooperation agreements with international crime syndicates that also took in the country's traditionally well-organized rings of smugglers. These rings, which connected India and Pakistan with the Middle East, earned large profits that each warlord increasingly threatened to confiscate by erecting road-blocks and charging tolls on through traffic.[55] In the 1990s, then, instead of the reconstruction of a regular economy, a link developed between the informal and criminal economies through which warlords and their armed followers were able to make a living. *Informal economies* are characterized by asymmetrical power structures in which the threat or use of force may at any time go unpunished, but community forms of self-organization (here, warlord forms) prevent the degeneration into a struggle of all against all.[56]

In the case of Afghanistan, this informal economy of the warlords was linked to the international criminal economy – something that is probably also largely true of Colombia.[57] But it does not have to be drugs or other illegal goods that link the robber economies of the transnational wars to the peace economies of neighbouring countries and the distribution circuits of the world economy; natural resources such as oil or iron ore, gold or diamonds, tropical woods or rare minerals are also suitable candidates. Consequently, an intra-state war tends to be more likely and more protracted the greater the minerals and other natural resources that can be sold to 'feed' and strengthen the warlords and militia leaders economically. Contrary to a view that is repeatedly argued, there have been cases where a

Afghan Mujahedin near Tora-Bora, December 2001
The wars in Afghanistan, stretching over two decades, eventually led to the collapse of all state structures. Here, too, the kalashnikov was an important combat weapon. It has become a symbol of the new wars, a robust and efficient token of male pride. Photograph: dpa.

country's better integration into the world market has by no means improved the chances of peace, but has mainly consolidated the position of warlords in control of certain minerals.[58] This has been especially true of the transnational wars in West and Central Africa.

The passage from closed to open war economies is mainly what distinguishes the new wars from the warlord configurations observable in nineteenth-century Latin America or in China in the first half of the twentieth century,[59] as well as from the classical model of civil war. Whereas classical warlordism rested essentially upon agrarian subsistence economies – drawing its resources from them through the spread of fear or, when necessary, overt displays of violence – the open economies that have taken shape in the last few decades prosper from a constant inflow of resources from abroad – whether the source is subsidies from other states, international corporations or wealthy émigré communities, aid supplied by international agencies, or income from strategic raw materials and, to some extent, illegal goods sold in the global 'shadow economy'.

The closed economies of classical warlordism did not pose a major problem for either international relations or the world economy. Since they could anyway maintain themselves for long periods only in peripheral and usually isolated regions, they disposed of limited resources and had a correspondingly limited sphere of influence. In terms of world politics, they were so marginal that they could be virtually ignored. It is true that the civilian population in a warlord-controlled zone often had to endure a regime of terror, but political or economic metastasis was not a feature of these war economies. On the contrary: if a regional warlord wanted to consolidate the foundations of his rule, his only options were to create a set of para-state structures or to take over officials and institutions (when still intact) from the state with which he had previously been at war. In other words, the warlord had a strong incentive to formalize and regularize the structures of force, and warring parties were usually aware that the war economy which they developed and exploited would be only a transitional phenomenon.

The decisive shift for world economy and politics occurred in the 1970s and 1980s in Peru and Colombia, when local guerrilla movements developed the perspective of stabilizing long-term informal rule over large territories. An essential condition for this was the creation of an open war economy, through association of the regional war economy with organized international crime. The growing and marketing of cocaine made such an alliance a real possibility.[60] Now this Latin American model has numerous imitators in Black Africa and Central Asia, especially as the end of the East–West conflict has meant that regional war players can hardly resort to the alternative way of building an open war economy – that is, reliance on a powerful 'third party' with the will and the interest to keep it going.[61]

In the framework of the East–West conflict, and with the later additional fuel of the political-ideological dispute between the USSR and China, closed war economies gradually turned into open war economies from the 1950s onward, as individual countries aligned themselves with either the Eastern or the Western bloc. They did not have to rely on the limited resources of the area under their military control but received a continual flow of military equipment and material aid, even if the country was of little strategic interest to the respective superpower and its allies. Unlike those war economies of the last decade that have been linked in to global circuits, these open war economies were placed under a certain degree of political control; the powers dominating world politics could influence the course of a war and the terms of a ceasefire, either by varying the flow of resources or, occasionally, by sending units of their own regular army (one example here being the Cuban intervention in the Angolan civil war[62]). This led to the idea that the conflicts were in fact 'surrogate wars', in which the decisive players were the superpowers and their alliance systems. But that was true only in a few cases. With the end of the East–West conflict, it soon became clear that many of the former recipients of ideological solidarity had themselves decided to extend the limited base of their war economy by laying hands on additional means for the pursuit of the war.

In the 1990s, in regions where strategic raw materials or valuable mineral deposits made it possible, the resource flows that used to take place within the framework of the East–West conflict were replaced with links mediated by the world market. International businesses – from the oil corporations to large-scale traders in diamonds, or even criminal organizations[63] – took over from a post-USSR that was unable, and a USA that was increasingly unwilling, to pay out the necessary sums. Although the influence that the superpowers had previously exerted over the course of war should not be exaggerated, there can be no disputing the fact that the economic basis underlying most of the wars in question now largely escaped the political control of other states and international organizations. The brief attempt to make up for the loss of direct political influence by means of embargo policies can now be seen to have failed.[64]

Probably, the emergence of open war economies no longer subject to outside political control has been the decisive factor lending the course of war its new independence. This does not mean that all wars over the past decade were funded entirely through links to a global shadow economy. Indeed, as before, a whole series were kept going through politically controlled resource flows: in Afghanistan, for instance, the Taliban could rely upon Pakistani and Saudi assistance, while the so-called Northern Alliance would scarcely have survived without Russian support. In a growing number of wars, however, there is no longer any discernible backing by 'interested third parties', and this political independence from outside forces makes wars funded through shadow globalization an increasingly attractive option for regional belligerents. Where no raw materials or mineral resources are available to be sold for this purpose, and where geographical or climatic conditions are not suited to the growing of poppy or coca plants, there is still the option of kidnapping women on a large scale and forcing them into prostitution in the brothels of the OECD world.[65] The strategy of sexual violence does not serve here to further a policy of 'ethnic cleansing', or to provide extra rewards for fighting men, but constitutes a means of funding the war that may be termed a revival of slavery.[66] Finally, as we have

seen, warlords and militia leaders can also use the media presentation of hunger and poverty to start up international relief supplies
of food and medicine from which their own fighters can be given
first choice. We may conclude, therefore, that scarcely any of today's
warlord configurations rests upon a closed war economy.

If warlords and warlordism were long seen as typical of stalled
modernization processes – in which the state had not (or had not yet)
achieved a monopoly on the legitimate use of force, but the old clan
and tribal structures no longer had the power to control it – the view
now is that warlords have been propelling a modernization process
of their own during the last two decades. They have emancipated
themselves from the specific social and economic structures to which
they used to be tied. Wars have become cheaper in the process of
economic globalization, and open war economies can be got up and
running fairly easily. Under these circumstances, the organized use
of force on a large scale and for a long period of time (which is
how war may be defined) has again become a lucrative proposition,
and this has crucially contributed to the extensive destatization and
privatization of war over the last two decades.

5

INTERNATIONAL TERRORISM

Terrorism as a communication strategy

The definition of terrorism is a matter of some controversy, for both factual and political reasons. Usually, the purpose in describing an act of violence as 'terrorist' is to deny it any political legitimacy; 'terrorism' functions in international politics as a term of exclusion. Those responsible for it are thereby told that no consideration will be given to their demands – at least so long as they employ certain forms of violence. For their part, organizations designated as terrorist often claim that they are waging a guerrilla war for the liberation of social or ethnic groups, and that the military superiority of the repressive forces compels them to resort to 'unconventional' methods. Problems arise with the term 'terrorism' not only because of objective factors but also because political players deliberately create semantic confusion to improve their own position and to worsen that of their adversary. Unless an influential political figure vigorously challenges the designation, anyone who is described as a terrorist over a long period of time will incur a major loss of legitimacy, whereas any group that manages to situate itself as a guerrilla organization within the international arena will have decisively advanced its political goals.

Although the word terrorism is today on everyone's lips, it is useful as a scientific category only if – beyond all semantic positional warfare – it successfully locates what is specific to certain economies and strategies of political violence and not to others. Furthermore, it is probably meaningful to speak of terrorism only if it can be identified as a means of forcibly imposing a political will: if it can be said to have an instrumental relation to the objectives of certain political players. In Clausewitz's definition of war as 'an act of violence intended to compel our opponents to fulfil our will',[1] there must exist a 'terrorist' political will to which we can ascribe decisions about the type and scale of the application of violence. This is not always immediately possible, however, since terrorist organizations operate in secrecy and with non-hierarchical networking structures; a political will must then ultimately be constructed and personalized in order to identify and combat the opponent. The Venezuelan Carlos and the Arab Osama bin Laden are examples of this. If such a will cannot be determined, it may be possible to speak of terror, but not of terrorism.

In general, terrorism may be described as a form of violence that mainly seeks to produce results in an indirect way. Terrorist strategies, then, are designed to generate *psychological* rather than directly *physical* effects; what counts for them is not so much the material damage caused by an attack – the scale of destruction, number of casualties, length of interruption to supplies – as the resulting fear and terror, and the hopes and expectations bound up with this that a seemingly overpowering enemy is vulnerable.[2] In this sense, terrorism has been characterized as a strategy for the spectacular communication of a certain kind of message.[3] In a variation on Clausewitz's description of battle as the measurement of the other side's moral and physical forces,[4] terrorism might be defined as a direct attack on the enemy's moral strength to impose the terrorist's will with a minimal level of physical forces. A direct confrontation with the enemy's physical forces, especially the armed forces, is thereby avoided, since it would in no way strengthen the attacker. In principle, the decision to initiate an armed clash with terrorist means is the result not of cowardice but of a rational evaluation of the relationship of forces.[5]

As we know, guerrilla fighters also operate in a situation where the enemy has superior forces at its disposal, and cohere they are in any event incapable of waging battle on an equal footing. But the use of force in partisan warfare is mainly intended to wear down the enemy's physical forces and thereby weaken its political will. Raids on minor positions and remote garrisons serve this purpose well, as do the destruction of railway lines or bridges and the blocking of mountain passes to disrupt supplies, or attacks on small troop detachments and, if possible, their encirclement and destruction in an area from which it is difficult to escape. The military success of such operations turns on the amount of material damage they cause, and so they must be repeated in numerous places if they are to have a visible effect on the adversary.

Partisan forces, though clearly inferior to the regular army both in numbers and in weaponry and training, must be sufficiently large to pose a persistent threat at several places at once. This is not the case with terrorists, however, whose number and weaponry do not enable them to mount guerrilla-style surprise attacks or to engage in brief clashes with regular army forces. Terrorists avoid such military encounters as a matter of principle, keeping their sights on the psychological rather than physical effects of their use of violence. The devastating bomb attacks on US military bases in Beirut and Riyadh were therefore terrorist rather than guerrilla actions, since their objective was not physically to weaken the troop units there but to send a message to politicians, and especially the public, in the United States. The one-off demonstration of the vulnerability of the US troops in Lebanon or Saudi Arabia was supposed to persuade the Americans to withdraw, without the need for a more protracted armed confrontation.

The message of a terrorist action nearly always has two addressees. First, those who are the direct object of attack are shown that they remain vulnerable and that their continued presence in the region (or, more generally, their persistence in a certain political course) will incur political costs in the form of material damage and losses. In principle, then, those behind the terrorist attack put the question whether the adversary is prepared to pay the same costs a second or a third time round, and they not unreasonably suppose that the enemy is not prepared to do so. This brings us back to Clausewitz's 'act of violence intended to compel our opponents to fulfil our will' – not, however, through destruction of the military means at the enemy's disposal, but through demonstrative acts of violence that aim to break its political will. The success of these is so much the greater the easier it is for the side under attack to withdraw without endangering its vital interests.

This is seldom the case, however – or else the government in question is simply not willing to allow small groups of people to blackmail it into changing its goals and objectives. Anticipating such a stance, every terrorist attack contains a further message that is designed to 'interest' certain 'third parties' (who are not the same as the 'interested third party' which, in Rolf Schreyer's and Carl Schmitt's usage, refers to the state ultimately backing and supporting a guerrilla war[6]). The message designed to 'interest' third parties is that resistance to what appears to be an infinitely superior power is not only possible but has good prospects of success, especially if more young men and women follow the lead of the initially small group and join the armed operations. The third parties, then, are those in whose interests the terrorists claim to be waging their struggle. According to its ideological orientation, the terrorist group may be fighting for the special rights or political independence of a certain ethnic or religious minority; it may be seeking to achieve the revolutionary emancipation of certain impoverished and politically marginalized layers within a country; or, finally, as in the case of militant Islamist groups, it may have taken up arms to restore the honour and self-respect of a religiously defined civilization.[7]

This third party, however defined, is not only the second addressee of the terrorist message but also an important source of legitimation. In their public statements and claims of responsibility, terrorist groups regularly evoke repression or discrimination directed against that third party as the real reason for their struggle, and they emphasize that they are fighting only to put an end to it. Terrorist attacks are nearly always a kind of staged threat, demonstrating to a particular state that it will face ever greater costs if it continues with its policy, but they are also an attempt to rouse a third party from its (supposed) political apathy or resignation and to motivate it for the armed struggle. The relative importance of the two messages varies from case to case. As a general rule, however, the one addressed to the target state counts for more if there is reason to think that the attack will induce it to give way, whereas the one addressed to the third party will count for more if the object of attack cannot give way and the aim of the struggle must be to wear it down and eventually destroy it. Whether it comes to that will naturally also depend on how the power in question responds to the attack. Its riposte may confirm the accusations against it in the terrorist claim of responsibility and push others to side openly with the author of the violent attack. But, if its countermeasures are sufficiently flexible, it may succeed in keeping a distance between the terrorists and the constituency they wish to involve in the struggle. As the initially weaker side, the terrorist group has to rely in the long term on the attraction and mobilization of that constituency if it is to succeed politically. This appears to be a notable difference between the key players in the new terrorist wars and the more traditional terrorists – from the Russian anarchists of the nineteenth century to certain violent formations of the far left in the 1970s and 1980s. The latter constantly have the third party in mind and start from the need to involve it actively in the struggle, whereas in the new forms of terrorism that third party must be not only activated but first produced as a political quantity.

From a tactic to a political-military strategy: the development of terrorism

Terror is nothing new in the history of politics, and from time immemorial it has been employed against repressive regimes and by resistance movements or attempted insurrections.[8] However, in the anti-colonial movements of the mid-twentieth century, which led in a short time to the collapse of European colonialism, terrorism reached an unprecedented level and, unlike the social-revolutionary terrorism of the second half of the nineteenth century,[9] achieved major political results.[10] Numerous political figures who appeared at the General Assembly of the United Nations in the 1960s had shortly before been branded and persecuted as terrorists; initially, they had mostly gained attention for themselves through terrorist attacks on the colonial power, and had nearly always stepped them up again when they found themselves in a tight corner militarily.[11]

In the Third World liberation struggle, terrorism proved its worth as a tactical component of guerrilla warfare, enabling small and weak organizations to demonstrate to a long-suffering or apathetic population that the mighty colonial power was actually quite vulnerable. Moreover, since official reprisals hit sections of the population that had until then been content with the colonial regime – or hoped for the gradual integration of local politicians into the administration – the result was to create a wedge between the population and the local politicians. It was by means of such terrorist attacks that the insurrectionary movements first drew in fresh fighters and gained the support of the population, both of which were necessary to start a guerrilla war with sufficient prospects of success. In the 1950s and 1960s terrorism became the detonator of guerrilla warfare. The tendency of terrorist groups to describe themselves as guerrilla forces dates from this period, when terrorists became partisans and partisans became heads of state.

As the detonators of guerrilla war, terrorist actions were limited to a brief phase of the liberation struggle and to a highly selective list of targets; they were not supposed to kill or injure anyone belonging to the social, ethnic or religious 'third party' whose involvement the terrorists sought to encourage. If this happened nevertheless, the group responsible would issue detailed explanations and excuses to prevent the adversary from using the victims in its propaganda. The politically legitimizing reference to a third party also ensured that no use was made of weapons of mass destruction or similar methods to maximize the consequences of violence, and that the arsenal remained limited to the traditional guns and bombs. Two developments marked a break with this self-limitation: namely, the internationalization of terrorism (which began in the 1960s but only really took off in the 1990s) and the use of religious-fundamentalist themes as an impetus and justification for terrorist attacks.

Of course, political or ideological limits on terrorist violence were fully accepted only by social-revolutionary and ethnic-nationalist groups. In the case of religious terrorism – which is by no means only Islamic but may also have roots among Christian or Jewish fundamentalists – the greater diffuseness of its constituency corresponds to a broader definition of the enemy beyond the ranks of the holders of political power. Thus, long before 9/11, terrorist groups with a fundamentalist motivation were already causing considerably higher casualties than social-revolutionary or ethnic-nationalist terrorism. As we have seen, religious-fundamentalist terrorism is not addressed to a third party in the hope of involving it in the struggle; at most it seeks to produce that third party through its own operations. It may further justify the use of violence by referring to millenarian or apocalyptic ideas that underline the restricted character of all earthly goals.[12] The fight against absolute Evil cannot take into consideration the possibility that some casualties might be innocent[13] – witness the poison gas attacks carried out by the Aum sect in the Tokyo subway, the bombing of government buildings in Oklahoma City, the blowing up of the US embassies in Nairobi and Dar es Salaam, and finally the devastating attacks on the World Trade Center in New York.

The internationalization of terrorism, beginning with the spectacular plane hijacks by Palestinian groups, also did a lot to remove the limits on violence. Even if the hijackers narrow the circle by releasing some potential victims at the first touchdown, the social and national composition of passengers in a civilian aircraft is much more unpredictable than the likely casualties of a bomb attack. The violence – by no means unintentionally, of course – becomes ever more diffuse and tends to be directed at any passenger in general, thereby giving additional prominence around the world to the hijacking incident. The effect is greater still when a terrorist group takes the further step of blowing up an aircraft, the most dramatic instance being the bomb over Lockerbie in Scotland that killed 250 people on a PanAm flight in December 1988. Internationalization of the terrorist groups themselves has further eroded the limits on violence, as ideological 'allies' with fewer scruples have joined in operations and shifted the implicit threshold. The most prominent example here was the rise of the Venezuelan Ilich Ramírez Sánchez – a man better

The hijacked 'Landshut' Lufthansa aircraft, 1977
For a time, international terrorists tried to use hijacks to draw attention to political issues and to force the release of imprisoned comrades. Here the 'Landshut' has landed in Dubai after its hijacking by Palestinian terrorists. Photograph: Ullstein.

known by his 'Carlos' alias – to become 'top terrorist' of the 1970s and 1980s.[14]

One change, scarcely visible at first glance, was the most momentous result of the internationalization of terrorism: namely, the revaluation of acts of terrorist violence from a preparatory tactic of guerrilla warfare to an independent political-military strategy, indeed to the operational focus of the 'war plan'. Whereas it had been considered politically essential to set clear boundaries to violence, these now inevitably receded into the background and the success of operations came to be measured by the resulting material damage, the numbers killed and wounded, and above all the intensity and duration of the media reporting of the incident. The rule now was: the greater the damage and the higher the number of casualties, the greater the impact and long-term success of the terrorist attack. The planners of 9/11 followed these new strategic rules of international terrorism.

The terrorist inversion of asymmetries of power

In the second half of the twentieth century, then, we may say that war successively freed a number of elements of violence from their tactical subordination to a genuinely military strategy.[15] The army's control over the various possible uses of force, as well as its capacity to integrate them as *tactical* options within the general strategic plan, depended essentially upon whether states were able to assert their monopoly on violence[16] and thereby limit the use of force in ways which, though cheaper in the short term, were more expensive and harder to control in the long term. This capacity of military strategy to control and subsume the application of force was a necessary precondition for the symmetrization of war. By contrast, asymmetry in the use of force goes together with the conversion of previously tactical elements of warfare into an independent strategic disposition. Whereas 'small war' (guerrilla warfare) used to be a concomitant of the 'large war', providing support and relief for the operations of the regular army, after the Second World War it gradually turned into a strategic option that was no longer necessarily subordinate to, or convergent with, a war fought by regular troops, as the theories of Mao Zedong and Ngyuen Giap had still conceived it.[17] The decisive innovations of guerrilla warfare took place not in China or Vietnam, or even in Cuba, but in the Middle East and North Africa – from where they spread to other regions where imitators were to be found. In this autonomization process, both military calculation and economic rationality played a key role. In the struggle against an external power, guerrilla fighters no longer had to think in terms of winning a war militarily; it was enough if they kept up the violence at a level that made the economic costs impossible for the enemy to sustain.

Similarly, in the last few decades terrorism too has developed into an independent strategy with no necessary connection to partisan warfare or other genuinely military modes of operation. Nor does it strike directly at the economy of the forces under attack, opposing its own determination and readiness for sacrifice to their guiding preoccupation with profit and utility. Rather, what is decisive for the new independence of terrorism is the association of violence with access to media coverage in the country under attack, so that a relatively small deployment of force can achieve the maximum effects.[18] Therefore, if the media density is insufficient or if news reports are subject to political censorship, terrorist strategies have little prospect of success; without the amplification provided by the media, their physical impact on the country's economic infrastructure would be too limited. (The attack on the World Trade Center is an exception in this respect, of course.)

The conversion of formerly subordinate tactical elements into an independent strategy therefore rests upon a major extension of the fields of conflict and a fundamental redefinition of the instruments of force. The monopoly on the means of war enjoyed by the armed forces, which was typical of Europe from the seventeenth to the twentieth century, is now a thing of the past. To put it most sharply, we might say that terrorism has changed into a global war of terror fought with no restrictions as to the choice of targets. In a parallel process, the civilian population and infrastructure have become crucial resources of war.[19] In partisan warfare, for example, the enlistment of at least logistical support from the civilian population is a fixed element of military planning and, where it is not given voluntarily, violence or the threat of violence may be used to achieve it. Only through increased mobility, concealment among the mass of non-combatants and reduced expenditure on supplies can guerrilla forces hope to offset the enemy's military superiority.

Guerrilla warfare revolutionizes the relationship of forces characteristic of classical warfare by converting the civilian population into a military resource from which only guerrillas (not regular armies) can profit. Faced with the technological superiority of the enemy's armed forces, the guerrilla fighter redefines the mode and location of battle and thereby acquires resources for war that are not available to the regular soldiery. Already Napoleon, under the impact of the Spanish guerrilla campaign, concluded that regular armies would have to adopt its new methods of warfare: that partisans could be fought only in the partisan style.[20] The result would be reprisals against civilians that could quickly escalate into massacres, as they did in nearly all counter-insurgency wars in the twentieth century. Redefinition of the mode and location of the use of force is also the reason why guerrilla wars are especially gruesome: if the regular army gets results by hitting at the civilian population, the guerrilla forces resort to similar means in order to avoid losing the support, cover and camouflage necessary to their survival. Initially, then, every guerrilla war is waged to secure the support of the civilian population, or to deny it to others.

Nevertheless, in military terms guerrilla warfare remains an essentially defensive strategy, even if it is politically employed for revolutionary objectives. There is a crucial difference between this and the strategy of terrorism, which in both political and operational terms has an essentially offensive character; it does not rely upon a favourably disposed civilian population for support, and may even discount it altogether as long as it is able to use its enemy's civilian infrastructure as a logistical base and a source of weaponry. This radical change in the mode and location of the use of force has introduced a new stage in the asymmetrization of violence. Bank robberies are one way of using the enemy's civilian infrastructure: the aim of these 'revolutionary expropriations' – such as Carlos Marighella advocated in his strategy of 'urban guerrilla warfare' and numerous terrorist groups practised in Latin America and Western Europe in the 1960s and 1970s – is to acquire the money to purchase weapons, accommodation and provisions for the terrorists. Plane hijackings are another example, which may not even involve use of the enemy's own infrastructure if the point is only to gain general attention or to blackmail other forces allied to the enemy or fighting on the same side. Finally, spectacular attacks on civilian persons and installations may sow lasting fear and terror in order to hit hard at economic life in the country under attack. This strategic redefinition of the instruments and locations of war reached its provisional peak on 11 September 2001.

The use of civilian infrastructure for terrorist objectives is all the easier and has all the greater impact, the denser are the transport and communications systems of the country under attack. The possibilities range from the posting of parcel bombs or anthrax letters through to attacks with computer viruses and other types of intervention in the enemy's systems of information and regulation. Terrorists may also gain considerable advantages by exploiting the political, legal and moral limitations that their target state imposes on itself; one of the terrorist calculations is that the other side will be unable to respond in kind and at the same level. It is therefore mostly post-industrial societies with a democratic constitution and a high media density that are singled out for attack. Agrarian societies, authoritarian or totalitarian regimes and countries with a low media density or perhaps even no national television are much harder to attack with terrorist methods. They remain locations for guerrilla warfare.

Even more than guerrilla warfare, terrorism is a strategy whereby militarily weaker forces – even the smallest groups – can engage in violent operations against large powers and superpowers. Only a minimum of funds are required to create a logistical base, to develop and deploy weapons, and to train and supply guerrilla fighters, and most of those funds come from outside the ranks of the terrorists themselves. This makes the adoption of terrorism and the launching of a terrorist campaign so easy and attractive in comparison with a guerrilla campaign, not to speak of a conventional war.

A further resource available for attacks on developed societies is the post-heroic mentality prevailing there, a mentality that terrorists deliberately counter with their gesture of heroic determination. Anyone who is prepared to sacrifice their life does not have to bother about escape routes and can concentrate all their energy on the attack itself. This makes the operation much easier to carry out, or in some cases possible in the first place, and considerably raises its prospects of success. Probably even more important, however, is the contempt for unheroic lifestyles in the target country that is expressed in such suicide attacks, for the psychological effects that they seek to achieve are dramatically intensified as a result. 'There is no protection from a suicide bomber': this common view among security institutions basically recognizes that terrorist operations are much more likely to be successful if the process of planning and implementation does not need to include a means of escape; but it also recognizes the symbolic power of a single-minded blow against the mentality of reconciliation and negotiation prevalent especially in Western societies, which are usually willing to buy their members out of mortal danger with money or political concessions. Thus, it is not only in their own eyes that the deadly resolve of suicide bombers constitutes a victory over the hated enemy, regardless of the actual consequences of the attack. Even if it is a failure, it remains a demonstration of resolve to which post-heroic societies react with confusion. The asymmetrization of forms of struggle in terrorism takes place at a symbolic as well as an instrumental level. Indeed, it is above all the symbolic dimension that is meant to create constituencies capable of being drawn into the struggle; this makes terrorist attacks a strategic element in the new wars.

As a general rule, of course, the systematic asymmetrization of violence through the use of terror at a strategic level is itself a response to military, economic, technological and cultural asymmetries so great that the inferior side has no chance of restoring symmetry through its own efforts. This kind of constellation has existed in the conflict between Israelis and Palestinians since the Six Days' War of 1967 and the Yom Kippur War of 1973, where it became clear – especially after Jordan and Egypt, the two most important neighbouring states, withdrew from the Arab war coalition – that Israel could not be defeated by conventional military means. Initial attempts to launch a guerrilla war had little success, but then the Palestinians increasingly turned to terrorist methods to achieve their political goals. This kind of regional asymmetry, which marked the Palestine conflict from the late 1960s onward, assumed global proportions in the early 1990s. Since the collapse of the Soviet Union no single state or coalition of states has been even remotely capable of matching the United States in symmetrical warfare, and none of the scenarios involving conventional armed forces would have been able to force it to change its policy in any fundamental way. This means that, for political players who do not accept US dominance or central aspects of US policy, there is no possibility of changing things – in a way that at least seemed conceivable in the perspective of the East–West conflict – through conventional military threats or alliance with a power able to issue such threats.[21]

The situation looks very different where asymmetrical strategies are developed to meet these asymmetrical constellations. The United States first learned this through the loss of the war in Vietnam, having proved unable to bring to its knees – politically and militarily – an enemy that used the strategy of guerrilla warfare to compensate for its technological inferiority in weaponry.[22] The vulnerability of American power was also evident in the military interventions in Lebanon and Somalia. In October 1983 commandos from the 'Islamic Jihad' terrorist group detonated bomb-filled trucks almost simultaneously at the headquarters of the US Marines and the French paratroopers in Beirut, killing 250 men at the former and more than 50 at the latter; Washington and Paris immediately decided to pull out their troops. And, ten years later to the month, a failed operation on 3 October 1983 to capture the Somali warlord Mohammed Farah Aidid in Mogadishu resulted in 18 dead and more than 80 wounded among the US soldiers (the mutilated and defiled corpse of one was filmed by CNN cameras as it was dragged through the streets);[23] once more Washington quickly withdrew its troops, even though they were part of a UN contingent that faced a difficult situation without them. Probably the events in Mogadishu were a key experience for Osama bin Laden and his strategists, who used them as a basis for the planning of later attacks by the al-Qaeda network.[24]

The media that repeatedly show such attacks, greatly amplifying events of slight military importance in themselves, ensure that – in a reversal of the conditions that obtained in Europe between the seventeenth and twentieth centuries[25] – the radically asymmetrical strategy of the new terrorist wars is given a special bonus. In asymmetrical warfare the media actually become a means of conducting the war. Those who have no capacity to attack the conventional forces of a certain state with any chance of success seek to disseminate images in which the consequences of acts of violence are made directly visible. A sense of horror is produced through recorded images, not only of violence against soldiers but also of violence used by the regular armed forces (for example, attacks on trains, housing or non-military factories and, most especially, the killing of women and children). Pictures of the latter kind, whether genuine or falsified, are meant to shake the good conscience underpinning the enemy's political will – the confidence (justified or unjustified) that violence is being used for a just cause. Pictures of the former kind attack the same political will directly, by confronting it with the price that will have to be paid; the assumption here is that the power under terrorist attack will in the long run be unwilling to incur such high costs. Pictures of acts of violence and their aftermath regularly include the message that next time the price may be even higher. Thus, the media-staged symbolic confrontation between, on the one side, small groups of utterly fearless and determined fighters and, on the other side, economically and militarily dominant states and societies marked by a post-heroic mentality is always itself an integral part of the struggle. Terrorism is a form of warfare in which combat with weapons functions as a drive wheel for the real combat with images. The transformation of war reporting into a means of warfare has probably been the most important step in the asymmetrization of war, the one which has made it possible to circumvent the military asymmetries of the 'new world order' – not through a restoration of symmetry, of course, but through the single-minded development of new asymmetries, such as those characterizing the new terrorist wars.

The target of terrorist groups: the fragile psychological texture of developed societies

The most important feature of the recent wave of international terrorism is this combination of violence with media presentation.[26] To put it sharply, terrorism is a strategy that uses violence to stage spectacular events through which certain messages are transmitted. Theoretically, terrorist groups act in accordance with principles similar to those of NGOs, which also stage events to draw attention in as spectacular a manner as possible to their core issues (for example, climate protection, child labour or the death of the forests). The images they produce are supposed to sensitize the international public to a particular issue, to put pressure on governments to take various measures and, not least, to publicize their own organization and thereby raise money among the population of the wealthy industrial countries. Terrorist groups – except in the case of action to force the release of jailed comrades – follow the same model. (To avoid misunderstandings at this point, it should be stressed that the analogy between certain NGOs and terrorist networks is limited to their use of the media for forms of spectacular self-promotion that are likely to arouse public attention and win support for their cause.) The spread of terrorism in the closing decades of the twentieth century was thus based not upon a revolution in the means of violence (the kind of revolution characteristic of the history of conventional warfare), but upon a media revolution that has fundamentally altered human behaviour in relation to information and leisure time. Terrorist operations are events with a high attention value, and in their case news in the classical sense has been replaced with images. With the production of spectacular images, the kind of written statement in which groups used to claim responsibility for the action and set out their motives and aims has become increasingly superfluous.

Evidently, the power of the media to amplify the effects of violence long restricted the scale of terrorist operations and, therefore, the amount of damage and the number of casualties that they caused. Until a few years ago most researchers assumed that dynamite and firearms (as already used by terrorists in the late nineteenth century[27]) would remain the favourite weapons of terrorist groups, and that these would consider the use of atomic, biological and chemical weapons of mass destruction neither tactically necessary nor politically attractive. This view has now changed.[28] Probably this has something to do with the need for larger and more devastating operations to penetrate the media hubbub, but a weightier factor appears to have been the declining significance of the third parties that were assumed to have an objective interest in the terrorist activity. So long as these constituencies were defined as the basis of social-revolutionary or ethnic-nationalist legitimacy, none of their members was supposed to come to harm as a result of any terrorist attack – a condition that totally excluded the use of weapons of mass destruction.

Things are obviously different in the case of religiously motivated terrorism, where a considerably broader definition of the enemy, stretching beyond functional and power elites to take in whole civilizations, goes together with a greater diffuseness of the third party to be involved in support of the terrorist group. These two factors together are probably the main reason why, for some years now, higher causalities have resulted from attacks perpetrated by groups with a religious ideology than by those with a social-revolutionary or ethnic-nationalist orientation.[29] The conjunction of religious motivation and terrorist strategy has meant that the spiral of violence twists up ever faster, since there is no longer a need for a third party as the basis of legitimacy to which the operation is addressed. God, or the Divine, provides legitimacy and perhaps even an addressee – or at any rate a reference – and requires no political calculation of the maximum damage and the maximum number of casualties that an attack must not exceed. As 9/11 showed, the need for ever more spectacular media effects and the religiously driven erosion of traditional limits on violence have come together in a deadly combination.

It is also a striking fact that terrorists with a religious hue increasingly forego the statement of responsibility that used to be common among social-revolutionary or ethnic-nationalist groups, preferring instead to rely entirely on the expressive power of images from the scene of the attack. This may be explained in terms of a kind of detachment of images from text. But the ultimate reason is that for such groups there is no longer an addressee in the world below to whom they feel accountable. The attacks of 9/11 are not the only proof of this, but they are the main one. If the terrorist 'message' is conveyed simply through images of the attack, without a background text explaining the action and setting out a list of demands, then we can no longer be sure what that message is. It could be a number of things, but its 'real' content and the 'real' aims of the groups behind it are shrouded in mystery. In the recent developments of international terrorism, this lack of clarity is certainly not a tactical deficiency – as it would be for social-revolutionary or ethnic-nationalist groups – but it is a central element in the strategic conception. The enemy is set a puzzle and left in the dark about the political ideas that fill the attacker's mind. Terrorist attacks that communicate their message purely through images, without a written statement in support, exclude in advance any compromise between the conflicting interests and objectives. Evidently they convey something other than a specific demand, which – whether a state granted it or not – would open the perspective of ending the campaign of terror. This aspect was apparent in the attacks of 9/11, but also in smaller subsequent operations by the same network, such as the gas tanker explosion in front of the synagogue in Djerba, Tunisia. So what are they supposed to achieve?

First, it is presumably conveyed to the objects of attack – in principle, anyone living or working in the Western world – that there will no longer be any security for them, at any time or anywhere; that the United States, despite its massive technological, economic and military superiority, is not capable of reliably and securely protecting its own citizens or installations. Obviously this message did not come across clearly enough, or was not taken seriously enough, after the massive explosions at the US embassies in Nairobi and Dar es Salaam, and so it was delivered again in the clearest possible way through the attacks on the Pentagon and the World Trade Center. The creation of a permanent threat was supposed to make the American people force their government into a narrowing rather than a broadening of the US global engagement. In addition to this basic political message, the attacks also involved an ever more intense appeal to the masses of the Islamic world, which should be seen as a residual figure of the 'third party to be won over to the struggle'. The spectacular demonstration of the vulnerability of the United States and its allies was supposed to make people in the Islamic world more confident that, despite the West's many-sided superiority, a wide-ranging, violent struggle against it was not without some prospect of success – provided that it did not employ conventional means to strike where the enemy was strong, but used other forms of warfare to strike where he was especially vulnerable. These are the two political messages that may be read from the attacks of 11 September 2001.

The strategists who planned the operations, however, probably did not regard these messages as so central. They would have speculated more on the economic and immediate political consequences, for their real target would seem to have been the West's easily broken web of economic expectations – its 'gambler's fantasy', as it were. Panic reactions were expected to occur among share dealers and investment managers, and indeed this is the fastest and most effective way of hitting societies that increasingly organize their economic life

The World Trade Center in flames, 11 September 2001
The latest form of international terrorism uses hijacked aircraft not as an instrument of political blackmail but as a quasi-military machine: a jet-propelled bomb. Photograph: dpa.

in the global dimension of stock exchanges. Here the damage resulting from terrorist attacks is the greatest, and – once the panic has
been sown in the stock exchanges – it is not limited to directly affected branches or sectors but rapidly extends to the whole economy.
Attacks on tourist facilities correspond to the same model, since they
can prompt economic decisions far more consequential than the immediate damage. Since countries heavily dependent on tourism may
be economically (and therefore also politically) ruined by spectacular attacks, they can often do nothing but bow to the pressure and
give at least indirect support to terrorist groups – for example, by
voting in a certain way in international organizations, by providing
shelter for hunted terrorists, by issuing political statements and pub-
licly taking sides, or by passing on information from secret services.
Terrorist groups have probably long been capable of establishing a
'protection money' system by means of carefully measured attacks
and credible threats of further attacks – a system in which political
support counts for more than the actual money. In particular, smaller
countries with a policy orientation to the United States and the West
can be quite easily (and above all cheaply) induced to make a change
of course, or anyway to adopt a posture not so closely aligned with
the West.

International terrorism, as it has manifested itself in recent years,
no longer uses violence as its only or even its preferred means of
conveying certain messages and information to the world public.
Unlike the various Palestinian groups of the late 1960s and early
1970s, which used spectacular hijacks to gain public attention for
their goals and demands, the new form of terrorist violence directly
targets the economic circuits of the Western world and the states
allied to it; its preoccupation with psychological rather than physical effects is precisely what identifies it as *terrorist* violence. It is
destructive not because it causes massive damage to a country's
infrastructure (its factories and shopping centres, its control and
transport systems), but because it sows terror and thereby tears the
fine psychological web of modern economies. This is the weakest
point of these societies, and it is a relatively easy one to hit.

MILITARY INTERVENTIONS AND THE WEST'S DILEMMA

War-fighting capacity and cost–benefit calculation

The dramatic rise in the costs of war, which include not only the preparation and deployment of fighting forces but the incalculable consequences of devastation in the home territory, means that war between states (especially between those with a highly developed economy and technological base) has been at least provisionally superseded as a historical model.

Nevertheless, the theory of democratic peace – that is, the general observation that democratic states have not waged wars against one another – is much less significant for an analysis of war in the twentieth century than most research on peace and conflict usually supposes.[1] In principle, it rests upon three simultaneous tendencies that are said to have reinforced one another and to have more or less overdetermined the peaceableness of democratic societies. These tendencies are *first*, the increase in the costs of war, which began with industrialization and continued at first gradually but then at an exponential rate; *second*, the parallel transformation of the guiding social model away from a craving for glory and honour towards purposive rationality; and, therefore, *third*, the development of institutional arrangements ensuring that this purposive rationality determines not only economic but also political decisions.

In the theory of democratic peace, political scientists working in the field of war studies have focused almost entirely on the last of these three tendencies and investigated the functional mechanisms of the democratic order as the all-decisive factor governing the inclinations of a society towards peace or war. Sometimes consideration is also given to cost–benefit calculation in international relations, and to ways in which it might be put on a reliable institutional foundation,[2] but this is not accorded a central role in the theory of democratic peace. In fact, the relevant studies nearly invariably – one might almost say systematically – leave out of account the enormous increase in the costs of war. Yet this has been the essential precondition for the effectiveness of the other two elements, and for the decline in the will and capacity to fight wars.[3] The directness of this correlation is shown by the fact that the scale and duration of the new wars mainly depend upon a dramatic lowering of the direct costs of warfare.[4] While peace and war studies have been seeking to devise institutional rules for a lasting peace, the strategists of violence have found ways and means of making war cheaper. In Germany, in particular, the hopes of experts in this field ended in failure and disappointment because they paid little or no serious attention to the internal economy of war. When they did focus on economic issues, it was with reference to the external interests and motives for which military force was supposed to gain recognition;[5] they did not discuss the extent to which soaring costs had made war prohibitively expensive.

The First World War made this a palpable reality, and first brought home the structural consequences for societies caught up in the cost explosion. The various powers entered the war with the expectation that it would be a brief engagement, rather like the European wars of the nineteenth century.[6] In the late autumn of 1914, however, it became clear that there would be no speedy resolution and that the conflict had turned into a war of attrition from which none of the belligerents would emerge the same as it had been before. This confirmed the prognoses of a number of non-military people – most notably, the Polish banker Johann von Bloch and the German-English industrialist and political writer Friedrich Engels – who had pointed to the huge costs and incalculable consequences of a protracted war.[7] When the First World War finally ended after more than four years, the three great powers dominating South-Eastern Europe and the Near East (the Tsarist, Austro-Hungarian and Ottoman empires) lay in ruins. But victors and vanquished alike faced the problem of rebuilding their economically and socially devastated countries: real national income had fallen by 10 to 20 per cent in Britain since the beginning of the conflict, by approximately a quarter in France, by 35 per cent in Italy and Germany, and by as much as 50 per cent in Hungary and Russia.[8] Out of every thousand men called up between the ages of twenty and forty-five, 187 had been killed in Hungary,

182 in France, 155 in Germany and 88 in Britain.[9] The middle layers fundamental to social cohesion and political-cultural orientation had been economically impoverished and politically radicalized.

It was now clear to all the former belligerent countries, with the possible exception of the relatively little affected United States, that none of them would be able to withstand another such war. The collapse of the Russian army, the refusal of French frontline divisions to take the offensive in 1917, the disintegration of the Austro-Hungarian army in the summer of 1918, the dwindling preparedness for battle of German troops after August 1918, the mutiny in the German deep sea fleet: all this plainly showed that even the limits of a population high on nationalist euphoria had been stretched to breaking point.[10] Between 1936 and 1939 Hitler politically exploited the horror of other European powers at the thought of another major war, and the Wehrmacht's sweeping military victories in the first years of the Second World War were due not least to the fact that no adversary was prepared to fight as unconditionally as a quarter of a century before. The collapse of the French army in the spring of 1940[11] demonstrated that democratic societies were no longer willing to assume the economic, social and human costs of such a war.[12] It is no accident that by and large the heaviest losses during the Second World War were borne in countries with totalitarian regimes: Nazi Germany and the Communist Soviet Union.

Three basic responses to the new situation emerged after the First World War. *First*, those who refused any form of military service, despite the legal and social sanctions against them, hoped that mass adoption of such a principled pacifism would make war an impossibility. *Second*, others hoped to construct an inter-state order that would prevent the outbreak of wars by means of international agreements and especially of international organizations such as the Geneva-based League of Nations. The outlawing of wars of aggression was a first step in this direction. *Third*, there was the option of trying to make it once more possible to fight a war. For those who took this course, it seemed that changes in strategy and combat tactics as well as the development of new weapons could eliminate the kind of war of attrition seen at Verdun or the Somme, and thus reduce the number of casualties on their own side and considerably lower the social costs of war.

The interwar period was typically one of unremitting struggle among advocates of these three responses, both at the level of individual European countries and in relations between them. Chamberlain's and Daladier's much-deplored policy of appeasement, culminating in the Munich agreement of autumn 1938 – whereby the Western powers sacrificed their political and military ally, Czechoslovakia, and forced it to surrender the Sudetenland to Germany – corresponded to the second of the above responses to the First World War. It was a last desperate attempt to maintain a peace in Europe on the basis of intergovernmental and international agreements and institutions; the attempt failed because Hitler wanted more than he could be given within such an order. War was on the cards by at least the spring of 1939, when German troops marched into what was left of Czechoslovakia, but the European powers were at stages of preparation for such a war that varied with the political and military conclusions they had drawn from the experiences of the 1914–18 conflict.

The matériel battles and the war of attrition that marked the First World War gave rise to three different strategies; these became the only possible ways of fighting a war between states, and together with guerrilla strategy and terrorist warfare they made up the five types of twentieth-century war. The three strategies in question were the offensive Blitzkrieg, the defensive Maginot-line doctrine, and an indirect approach ranging from economic blockade to strategic bombing. However much they may have differed in details, all shared the underlying assumption that war should be fought only if it was expected to be brief and to involve much fewer military losses than before, the aim being that the effects on their civilian population could be kept within narrow bounds.

The *Blitzkrieg strategy*, mainly worked out by younger officers in the German Reichswehr, postulated that a long drawn-out war of attrition could be avoided through the strengthening of the army's offensive capacity and its deployment over a smaller area. In keeping with the principles of Napoleonic strategy, it was their aim to make the battlefield once again the place where the war was decided. After Germany's Schlieffen Plan and France's planned push through the Ardennes and across the Rhine both failed to achieve success in 1914,[13] the decisive terrain for the course of the war shifted from the battlefield to the economies of the two alliance systems. This relocation meant that the military recovered its function as the dominant and controlling force of war, and that the influence held by civilians and economic experts since the autumn of 1914 was now curtailed. Motorized, armour-led units with huge firepower, supported from the air by the 'flying artillery' of fighter-bombers, were now supposed to break through the front and push deep into the hinterland, turning the enemy forces from the rear and cutting their supply lines. In the end, the Blitzkrieg army would encircle the enemy and force him to surrender, without being caught up in long battles and incurring heavy losses.[14]

The Wehrmacht in the early part of the Second World War, the Israeli army during the Six Days' War and finally the US-led invasion force in the 1991 Gulf War applied this strategy with relative success. In each case, however, they were ultimately unable to convert rapid military victory into lasting political gains; the military achievements remained precarious because they were not recognized politically by the inferior side. In any event, a militarily successful application of the Blitzkrieg strategy presupposes high-quality equipment, well-trained and highly disciplined troops and an officer corps ready and willing to take decisions – which all makes the preparation of such a war hugely expensive. That Blitzkrieg will fail if one of these elements is missing may be seen from the experience of the Iran–Iraq war, when the Iraqi armed forces were unable to break decisively through the Iranian frontline, and the conflict – like the First World War in Europe – went on to be fought as a war of position that brought heavy losses as each side tried to wear the other down.[15]

Whereas the Blitzkrieg strategy sought to avoid a war of attrition or exhaustion by strengthening the offensive capability of the armed forces, the *Maginot doctrine* aimed at the exact opposite: to strengthen the defensive forces by making them as invulnerable as possible. In a sense, this solved the problem of the war of attrition by distributing its costs in an asymmetrical manner: the attacker was supposed to incur intolerable losses, while those on the defending side would be kept so low as to be politically manageable. This conception, mainly implemented in France under War Minister André Maginot,[16] took shape in the form of a huge fortified belt of steel and concrete that was supposed to defend frontline troops from any attack: the so-called Maginot Line. Militarily, however, scarcely any of these defensive ideas fulfilled the hopes invested in it – either because the losses on the defending side were considerably greater than expected, or because the attacker made strategic use of its greater mobility to cancel out the advantages of defence. Recent discussion of US plans for a strategic missile defence system brings home to us how deeply mythical ideas of the hero (made invulnerable by dragon's blood or the like) entered into the Maginot doctrine and similar conceptions.

The third, and probably the most momentous, political-military consequence of the First World War experience was the *strategic air war*, as conceived especially in Britain after 1940.[17] In principle, this was a variant of the 'indirect approach' that had become characteristic of Britain's navy-supported warfare by, at the latest, the time of

British soldiers returning to a French fort, 1939
The French response to the First World War experience was to strengthen
the defensive. Bunkers and fortified towers capable of withstanding heavy
artillery fire were supposed to reduce the intolerable losses that had become
associated with a war of attrition. Photograph: Ullstein.

the Napoleonic Wars. Winston Churchill pursued this strategy in its
traditional form at the beginning of both the First and the Second
World War. His idea was that, in order to avoid high casualties at all
costs, the enemy should be attacked not at its strongpoints (where
the bulk of the forces were concentrated) but at its 'soft underbelly' –
that is, the largely unprotected supply lines for such essential goods
as oil, gas or rubber, and, above all, the militarily weak or politically
indecisive allies from whom no great resistance was to be expected.

Examples of the traditional form of 'indirect approach' are the
landing of British, Australian and New Zealand troops on the
Gallipoli peninsula in 1915 (to hit at the Ottoman ally that was so
crucial to the Central Powers) and the landing of British troops in
northern Norway in spring 1940 (with the aim of cutting the flow
of Swedish iron ore to Germany). Both operations ended in failure,
however. The strategic air war, which Churchill announced long before the RAF was really in a position to launch it, was aimed not
at the supply lines to the enemy's economic centres but above all at

the supply of labour for the arms industry. To change the image, we might say that it was not the soft underbelly but the skeleton and nerves which were the main object of attack; contact with the enemy's mailed fist was still being avoided. Of course, the shying away from decisive battles and the systematic bombing of industrial centres and workers' districts meant an end to the distinction between combatants and non-combatants that had come with the statization of war.[18] Military force was now consciously and deliberately directed against the civilian population.

It was mainly the Western powers that developed this form of strategic air war in the second half of the Second World War, using it against both Germany and the Japanese Empire.[19] The dropping of atom bombs on Hiroshima and Nagasaki was only the climax of an air war against Japanese civilians that was supposed to force a surrender without the need to risk the loss of Allied ground troops in the struggle for the islands. This strategy was followed up in the B–52 bombing of Vietnam, and a more sophisticated variant was employed in the attacks on Serbian water and electricity installations as well as television stations during the Kosovo war of 1999. Here, too, the target was not enemy armed forces but the political will of the population to resist, and technological developments meant that this could be broken not through the destruction of workers' districts, as in the Second World War, but through the destruction of key utilities. There are a number of reasons to suppose that the main intention of these attacks was to force the Yugoslav government to give way over Kosovo.[20] The requirement in all such aerial operations, including most recently in Afghanistan in the autumn of 2001, has been the avoidance of casualties on the side that launches them; the governments in question assume that heavy losses could not be demanded of their own people and would soon lead to rejection of the policy of military intervention. To meet such requirements, account has also been taken of so-called collateral damage among civilians in the country under attack, and the political and military leadership has been visibly at pains to keep these within certain bounds.[21]

The same principles and mechanisms that forced war into a subordinate position within the repertoire of Western democracies has finally led to a situation where – if they do after long hesitation decide on military intervention in a conflict (either to prevent violence by the sides in a civil war, to protect human rights or to destroy terrorist bases) – they can deploy only their air force or sea-based missiles or, at most, small specialized units. The well-known reluctance to send in ground troops is offset by limitless faith in the military potential of so-called air strikes.

The law of democratic peace, more accurately defined, should be that democracies are incapable of waging symmetrical war, because a population that pursues its own interests and influences political decisions through its voting behaviour has not been willing, since the First World War, to accept the high losses predictable in such a conflict. On the other hand, democracies are perfectly willing to enter into asymmetrical wars, provided that they do not incur excessive casualties or economic damage. After 1945 France, Britain and the United States fought a whole series of such wars against resistance movements or dictatorial regimes.[22] It is likely, however, that the internal politics of the enemy country was not as decisive as in the asymmetrical conflict situation, which meant that the war could be expected to end in a swift victory with no major losses.

The model for all these wars was the battle of Omdurman on 2 September 1898,[23] when a British expeditionary corps under Lord Kitchener used its technological dominance – in the shape especially of the newly deployed machine-gun – to annihilate a numerically far superior force of Arab-Sudanese fighters called in by the Mahdi of Omdurman and sustained no noteworthy losses of its own.[24] Strictly speaking, Omdurman was not a battle but a massacre. The British machine-gun defences never even came within range of the Arab-Sudanese troops, who were unable to cover the intervening ground and fell bleeding to death in their thousands. Less than twenty years later, the gun that had assured the superiority of one side at Omdurman was more evenly distributed on the battlefields from Flanders to the Vosges,[25] and the introduction of other new weapons systems no longer changed the course of battles. During the First World War, neither side could achieve such technological superiority in weapons as the British had gained at Omdurman and in many other massacres of the colonial wars.

In the second half of the twentieth century, the means of establishing such superiority shifted from the battlefield to the skies, from ground troops to the air force. The reason for this was the growing use of partisan tactics, as a result of which European and American forces were unable to cash in their technological lead and found that the logistical expenditure associated with new ground-based weapons systems was their Achilles heel.[26] Partisans left their mighty enemy punching the air and moved into the hinterland to attack less well-armed and more vulnerable reserve units. The preference for air power mainly stems from the fact that its instruments are out of the enemy's reach: both during the operation, when the aircraft fly too high to be reached by ground fire, and between operations, when they can use aircraft carriers or remote bases. The often-used

term 'surgical strike' is here quite apt: any form of symmetry is eliminated, as one side is laid out on the operating table and the other
side busies itself with the instruments it considers appropriate. A
key difference from the actual practice of medicine is that, in the
political-military imagery of intervention, not only is the 'patient'
not asked for his or her consent to the operation; he or she is also
nearly always incapable of paying for it. The surgeon has to meet the
costs of the operation and the aftercare (which can sometimes last a
very long time) and so is anxious to keep them from escalating out of
control. If the patient is also likely to put up strong resistance to the
treatment, the operation may not go ahead – regardless of whether
it is indicated or not. In other words, although Western democracies
are quite prepared to involve themselves in the armed pacification
of whole regions, their decision depends not on whether all other
options to end a war have failed but on whether the funds can be
found for such an operation and whether it is consistent with their
own interests. Only where the situation is as asymmetrical as in the
surgeon–patient image are the Western democracies willing to intervene. If they have to face the possibility that the other side is capable
of reacting to the asymmetrical situation with its own strategies of
asymmetrization,[27] then they will give up any plan to intervene.

Demands for intervention to protect human rights and to end civil wars

After the end of the East–West conflict and the break-up of the Soviet
Union, a policy of military intervention took shape. Some celebrated
this as the beginning of a new world political order, while others
saw it as a new form of colonialism or an imperialism in humanitarian disguise that had to be vigorously combated. The concept
of a 'global domestic policy', which first appeared in the 1980s and
was supposed to express the end of the old forms of intergovernmental foreign policy and international wars,[28] was also interpreted
in various ways. For some, it provisionally marked the final state
of a desirable political order, in which human and civil rights were
guaranteed in principle and massive violations were punished with
police-type measures. Under the impact of the NATO intervention
in Kosovo, Jürgen Habermas described the humanitarian military
action as 'pure anticipation of a future cosmopolitan state that it also
seeks to promote'.[29] For critics of any policy of armed intervention,
such as Noam Chomsky, the reference to human rights was nothing

other than a blank cheque for the United States to intervene militarily whenever and wherever it pleased, in pursuit of its own geostrategic and economic interests.[30] The Munich sociologist Ulrich Beck, for his part, has tried to combine the positions of both sides by talking of a new era of 'postnational wars' in which 'the classical distinctions between war and peace, internal and external, attack and defence, justice and injustice, killers and victims, civil society and barbarism' are blown apart, and human rights policy becomes a kind of civil religion of the West, especially the United States.[31] Beck, therefore, expects that traditional international law, which rested upon nation states as the main political players, will be gradually supplanted by 'a global domestic policy' that involves 'a new kind of postnational politics of *military humanism*' – hence 'the use of transnational military power with the aim of enforcing the observance of human rights across national frontiers'. But this tendency, which for Habermas is so welcome, Beck immediately dips in the vinegar of Chomskyan critique: 'The good news is the bad news: the hegemonic power decides what is right, what is a human right. And war becomes the continuation of *morality* by other means. Precisely for this reason, it becomes all the more difficult to put a stop to the logic of military escalation.'[32] Beck's prognosis, then, is that the twenty-first century will see an ever-growing number of pacification and human rights wars.

In their expectations, warnings and prognoses, however, none of these three authors has looked carefully at the economics of war and asked under what conditions the state, even a superpower, will assume the major costs and risks of a military intervention whose success will mainly be of benefit to others. Those who are opposed in principle to such interventions maintain that their purpose is not to help the victims of civil war and human rights violations, but rather to assert the interests of the states that carry them out. For Habermas, on the other hand, it is evidently beyond doubt that there are state and supra-state actors who are able and willing, if necessary with military force, to pursue the collective good of global human rights, without especially profiting from it themselves. For his part, Beck assumes that they do profit from it when he speaks of a power-political hegemonization of human rights policies. But none of the three calculates the costs and risks that a state assumes when it declares itself to be the guarantor of human rights. Chomsky's acerbic critique of US foreign policy is ultimately based on the observation that the United States is unwilling, either today or in the future, to let itself be made the instrument of a worldwide human rights policy, that it appeals to such principles only when this is consistent with its particular interests and that it otherwise forgets all about its human rights policy. It would appear, then, that the main problem with recent debates about the rights and wrongs of military intervention is that they approach it from the point of view of the interventionist party and pay only marginal attention to the area where the intervention actually takes place. Instead of abstract discussions of legal and moral philosophy, objections arising from the critique of imperialism or general theses on changes in the world order, a political-theoretical analysis should start from the dynamics and escalatory mechanisms of intra-societal and transnational wars.[33]

If we bear in mind the dynamics of civil wars and, in particular, the three main characteristics of intra-societal wars – loss of time and devaluation of the future, marginalization of peaceful skills and overemphasis on violent capabilities, and the formation of interests bound up with the civil war – then it becomes clear why such conflicts only very rarely end with the negotiation and implementation of a political compromise between the two sides. Much more often they last for years and do not peter out even as a result of the increased use of resources; the allocation of prospecting and drilling rights for mineral resources and the trade in illegal goods link the wars to the world economy, which provides the wherewithal for them to continue.[34] Through this association with a globalized economy, such wars pose a long-term threat to the peace economies of nearby and even faraway countries. It is for this reason above all that other states, alliances or the United Nations may decide to try to end the war with the help of armed force. The logic of such interventions is mainly based not on human rights considerations or cosmopolitan legality,[35] but on political-economic calculation as to whether the costs that a continuation of the war will inflict on other countries are likely to be appreciably greater than the costs of military intervention. Along with the problems that arise from links between civil war fighters and international organized crime, the calculation must also take into account refugee flows caused by intra-societal and transnational wars – particularly, of course, in so far as this affects the countries that have to serve as hosts. At a certain point human rights arguments may begin to play a role, but they alone are probably never the driving force behind a decision to intervene; the key factors are political and economic, although – contrary to the assumptions of the theory of neocolonialism or imperialism – it is mostly a question of defensive rather than offensive interests. The interventions around the turn of the twenty-first century, unlike those of classical colonialism or imperialism, have served not to spread an economy of plunder but to roll back and restrict one that already existed.

The new intra-societal wars and civil war economies pose various threats to the peace economies of other countries. *First*, the conflict may spread to neighbouring countries – a fairly regular occurrence, unlike in the traditional boundary wars between states.[36] Parties and groups in temporary difficulties may try to escape strong military pressure by moving to the territory of a nearby country, or at least by establishing rear bases and supply depots there for long-term use. An intra-societal conflict may thus turn into a transnational war that spreads out in ever wider circles, so that it becomes increasingly difficult to get the different sides together for negotiations and tie them into a peace process. Even the scope for ending the war through outside military intervention becomes ever narrower as it acquires a transnational character. It would, therefore, appear that such a spiral should be halted as early as possible, if necessary through military intervention, while the risks and likely duration of such an operation are still more or less calculable.

A *second* threatening element in civil war economies stems from their association with organized international crime. Illegal goods traded by the warring parties, as well as the routes used to circumvent embargoes of the international community, develop and consolidate the links by means of which civil war economies force their way into the peace economies of neighbouring countries. The stronger and more persistent this influence becomes, the greater are the problems for the stability and functioning of the peace economies; the share of the criminal economy in the peace economy may grow by leaps and bounds, and it is not easy to combat international crime because it can withdraw into areas controlled by warlords, local militias or guerrilla groups where Interpol is powerless to act. The same is true of international terrorism, whose favoured locations for training camps and rear bases lie in areas where the state structures have collapsed in the course of an intra-societal war. The fact that such regions may become a target for military intervention, even if they are of no major geostrategic or economic interest, refutes the claim that the intervention policies of recent years are imperialist in nature; it also shows that, in a globalized world, there are no longer any regions where the state structures can collapse without triggering grave consequences for the world political and economic order. The importance of these regions for drug cultivation, as well as for the recruitment and training of terrorist units, means that even a careful cost–benefit calculation would suggest military intervention or massive military aid for a state threatened with collapse.[37] Undoubtedly, such measures are by no means guided only by the standards of a human rights policy. The double standards frequently deplored in

US foreign and military policy, whereby human rights may be actively enforced in one case and given the lowest priority in another,[38] have their roots mainly in economic and political considerations that are often hard to square with a policy geared to human rights.

Third, in the decision to go for military intervention, the dominant interest may be to forestall a certain kind of learning process. This applies especially when one power in a politically unstable region gains considerable advantages over its neighbours by driving out whole sections of the population, exporting tensions and conflicts, and reorganizing its own state on an ethnically homogeneous basis. If it succeeds in this 'ethnic cleansing' policy without encountering massive resistance from the international community, other power-oriented politicians in the region may be encouraged to play the 'ethnic card' on the next occasion as a way of building up support among the favoured population group; the policy may then spread like wildfire and destabilize the whole region. In this way an intra-societal conflict may rapidly turn into a transnational war that can no longer be circumscribed or controlled. To nip this in the bud is a good reason for neighbouring states, or an alliance system guaranteeing regional stability, to act swiftly and decisively against such a policy of 'ethnic cleansing'. NATO's decision to intervene early and massively in Kosovo – unlike in Bosnia, where it hesitated for a long time – was at first mainly an attempt to put the ethnic card out of play. Of course, human rights arguments were also relevant for the decision – not least for the public debate within the countries that launched the intervention, where they served to downplay the international legal principle of non-interference in internal affairs[39] – but they would not have been the decisive factor.

In this connection, the growing influence of the media on political decisions should not be underestimated. Just as media reports of losses among the intervention forces or 'collateral damage' may whittle down public support for the policy and eventually lead to its rejection, so can accounts of human rights violations, massacres, rapes, stray children and so on ensure that society in the interventionist country is willing to bear the costs and risks of sending in troops. Struggle over which images are deemed to be 'correct' is thus always also a struggle for popular support or rejection of an interventionist policy. Not surprisingly, the broadcast images and reports should be treated with suspicion, as they by no means always give an accurate picture of the situation on the ground.[40] It is true that the scale and forms of wartime deception may not have fundamentally changed since the age of classical inter-state conflicts, and that 'black propaganda' and the suppression of reports of atrocities have always existed. What has changed is the importance of this policy of lies and deception. In the form of media influence over the public, it also affects fundamental policies: television paves the way for the final decision to intervene or not to intervene. No real *arguments* are presented in support of a human rights policy; rather, strong emotions of revulsion and sympathy are mobilized to reduce the normally dominant effects of cost–benefit calculation.

The three reasons just given for early and decisive intervention to head off the threat of another new war in regions of crisis and conflict stand opposed to the definite aversion of Western societies to the associated military costs and risks. These societies initially prefer to adopt a wait-and-see policy, in the hope that the political and financial burdens of an impending intra-societal war (refugee flows, a burgeoning informal and criminal economy, imitation of certain strategies in other countries) will be less onerous than the costs and risks of military intervention. The post-heroic mentality of much of the population in the Western democracies already ensures that a policy of humanitarian military intervention will not turn around into the kind of imperial expansion that marked the history of the eighteenth, nineteenth and early twentieth centuries.[41] If neo-imperial practices exist on a world scale, they manifest themselves in credit policies – the presence (or absence) of international corporations and the sending of so-called military advisers – more than in a policy of military intervention to end intra-societal wars.

The character and political costs of strategies to minimize military risks

Why is it always mainly troops from Western states that are used in military interventions? Why are these expensive units not replaced with considerably cheaper forces from countries directly adjoining a war zone, forces that are more familiar with the climatic and geographical features and therefore probably less likely to incur losses. The question may also be formulated in a rather more provocative manner. Why is little or no use made here of the normal strategy for the lowering of production costs; that is, the use of cheaper labour, either by bringing it in from abroad or by relocating production in a low-wage country? Of course, Third World countries have always supplied large contingents for UN operations, the most notable being India and Pakistan, which had a long military tradition of their own before it was reshaped by the British. The real problem, however, is that the armed forces deployed to end intra-societal wars must be highly disciplined and resistant to corruption – otherwise, they will soon become part of the civil war themselves and succumb to the offers and suggestions of the burgeoning war economies. The deployment of Nigerian troops in the civil war in Sierra Leone is one especially dramatic example of what can go wrong when a UN-mandated intervention falls into this trap. The warring parties were well provided with funds, and it did not take them long to corrupt the new arrivals and even to buy up their weapons and ammunition. The Russian army in Chechnya does not seem to have performed much better, although in this case it was not an outside force sent in to bring peace to the region but one of the parties in the conflict. It proved to be corruptible, from ordinary soldiers right up to top officers, and this is probably the main reason why, despite its over-whelming strength within a small geographical region, it has not yet managed to bring the war to a successful end.[42]

At the turn of the century, then, a fast-rising number of war zones stand opposite a small number of powers that are capable of inter-vening but are rarely willing to do so because of their particular interests and political constitution. There is an ever greater need to nip new intra-societal wars in the bud by sending in forces from outside, but the scope for this has not increased but rather tended to shrink;[43] this is another reason why new wars have spread with-out hindrance in recent years and why the trend will be difficult to reverse in the near future.

OECD governments think of military intervention more as a way of exporting conditions for political stability than as the actual pro-vision of the basic prerequisites of statehood. Political stability is a collective good which directly benefits societies threatened or al-ready ravaged by intra-societal war, but in the medium to long term it also benefits all other countries. Habermas's and Beck's vision of a dawning age of global humanitarian politics, in which interven-tion puts a stop to major violations of human rights, is unrealistic because there is no consensus about how the costs should be shared; and OECD states, despite their wealth, would probably not have enough to meet the costs even if they were willing to pay them. Be-sides, it is extremely cheap to start up a new war[44] – especially if it is fought with the methods of international terrorism – whereas interventions to export political and in some degree economic sta-bility are rather expensive, the more so if they require a long time to produce results. Germany, for example, with its military interven-tions in the Balkans, the Horn of Africa and Afghanistan, is already stretched to its limits, and it is by no means alone in bearing these burdens. In short, the expectation of a new and peaceful world order after 1989–90 has long since foundered on the enormous costs of its creation. Once it became clear how high these costs really were, and how few governments were able and willing to assume them, the readiness for war-ending, peace-making intervention fell away from the point to which it had risen in the previous decade.

Still more serious than the financial burdens of intervention are the political risks associated with them for the Western democracies. Each government must reckon with the possibility of major losses, and public support tends to dissipate with every fresh report of soldiers killed or wounded. To lower this risk, if major resistance is expected on the ground, the intervention is at first limited to air strikes and sea-based cruise missiles, which, unlike ground troops, can bring fully to bear the technological superiority of the Western armed forces. The use of precision-guided weapons thus changes the nature of warfare itself, by overcoming the unity of killing and dying embodied in the classical type of soldier; it creates an uneven distribution of killing and dying that goes considerably beyond the battle of Omdurman. The pilot of a fighter-bomber or the crew of a warship equipped with Tomahawk missiles is outside the range of enemy fire. Here war sheds all the features of the classical duel situation and, to put it cynically, approximates to certain kinds of pest control. The deployment of such systems therefore constantly threatens to turn combat operations into a massacre, and the thin line between the two is maintained only by accurate targeting and by the work of international legal officers in monitoring the choice of targets.[45] The classical army ethos, which for a long time was probably the most reliable obstacle to the conversion of fighting into massacre, has been supplanted by a combination of technical precision and legal control.

The portrayal of this imbalance in the media often makes intervention appear morally dubious, with the result that public support and party positions may change. Air strikes must not continue beyond a relatively short period of time. If they do, the whole intervention project may quickly become politically discredited: influential politicians begin to speak up vociferously against the bombing, the peace demonstrations grow larger and so on. Considerable political costs therefore have to be set against the lowering of military risks – and those costs increase if the air strikes cause a large number of civilian casualties. It may also be assumed that the side under attack will try to circulate (genuine or false) pictures of civilians killed in the bombing in order to offset the military pressure with political pressure of its own.

B–52 bomber in action
The strategic air war has become the model most widely used by rich countries with a democratic form of government. Its aim is to inflict major damage on the enemy and thus make him submit politically, while largely avoiding losses on the side that carries out the bombing. Photograph: Popperfoto/Alamy.

But it is not only pictures of stray bombs that threaten to nullify the effect of an intervention mainly resting upon air strikes; often it is not at all clear what the bomb and missile targets should be. A functioning infrastructure of water and electricity installations, television stations and so on does provide identifiable objects to be attacked and destroyed, but very few may be left if years of civil war have already left the country in ruins. In that case, little political pressure can be brought to bear, and the side under attack can wait with a certain calmness for the bombing to stop by itself – at the latest when it becomes generally known that the material value of the bomb loads and missiles is several times greater than that of their targets. The attempt to minimize the political-military risks through the use of air strikes and precision-guided weapons once again brings out the asymmetry of the new wars. For, whereas their main players can profit from the cheapening of war, the interventionist powers continue to be faced with the rising costs typical of the history of classical warfare. In the end, this tendency will probably reach a point where the strategy of air strikes can no longer be employed.

The alternative to hi-tech intervention is the use of mercenaries, whose military losses are of lesser political consequence. By mercenaries, we should understand all those who, in terms of citizenship, do not belong to the electorate of the country behind the military intervention and therefore have no voice in a system calculated to be politically responsive. Their provision of humanpower, the fact that they expose themselves to the possibility of bodily harm and loss of life, is rewarded only with military pay and involves no political tie of any kind. In the history of political thought, this lack of political ties to the contractor has again and again been viewed as the crucial defect of the mercenary system. In modern 'post-heroic' societies with a high degree of political responsiveness, however, this suddenly turns out to be a major point in its favour. Mercenaries, unlike professional soldiers or conscripts originating in the national electorate, have no possibility of eliciting a political response in the event of high-risk and high-loss operations.

The recruitment and deployment of mercenaries may involve two different sets of duties and obligations. Either the mercenaries become regular troops in an army even though they are not citizens of the country in question – the case of the French Foreign Legion, for example, or the British Gurkha units – or they offer their services as 'freelancers' on the globally networked labour market, which is studied not only by private individuals and large companies but also by the governments of Western democracies. Though highly questionable both politically and morally, the freelance role without doubt provides the best avenue for the minimization of risks and the lowering of costs, and there is abundant evidence that a number of Western governments, especially that of the United States, have turned to it for minor covert interventions. It is quite another matter whether this kind of soldier is the best suited for operations designed to end a war and to bring peace; 'freelancers' can scarcely be expected to have the discipline and incorruptibility that are an essential condition for the success of such interventions. In the short term, however, they can certainly be effective in solving the problems of the state that organizes the intervention: their increased use may both reduce the associated political risks and check the tendency for the costs of war to keep spiralling upwards. Furthermore, the recruitment of mercenaries fits in most closely with the 'free market' mentality of post-heroic societies. It is true that a continuation of this tendency would have enormous political consequences, as the armed force would be subject to weak control by governments (linked only by the employment relationship). The impetus for the privatization of war would then come not only from the war zones and impoverished regions of the world, but also from the heartlands of power and prosperity. Privatized warfare would rapidly take on a disastrous life of its own, in accordance with the laws of the market.

Challenges facing security policy

As a result of the trends described above, the tasks of a security policy have dramatically altered in the last ten to fifteen years. They have become more complex and unclear, but the main change is that new asymmetries have appeared to challenge and replace the old symmetries upon which security policy used to be based. Not only did inter-state war make complex situations clear and militarily resolvable because of the symmetry of the belligerents; the sovereignty principle programmed the whole international political order for symmetry. This has now changed with the return of semi-state private and partly commercial players – a process accelerated by the development of a global political order in which it is not symmetries but asymmetries that dominate. It was an illusion to think that the end of symmetrical wars also marked the end of wars *tout court*. For the asymmetrical wars that have taken their place will determine the history of the twenty-first century.

Today inter-state war is an out-of-date model, and so too perhaps are the international legal norms associated with it, which mainly refer to individual states. Whereas Europeans are for the moment still trying to develop the existing body of international law and to adapt it to the changed conditions of world politics, the Americans have begun to bid a gradual farewell to it. Two signs of this are that the United States refuses to recognize an international jurisdiction with the power to punish war crimes, and that American intellectuals from various political backgrounds propagate the idea of just wars. The European way may be seen as an attempt to restore the minimum prerequisites for symmetrical politics, while the American way is leading in the direction of asymmetry. Which of these two proves the correct course will mainly depend upon whether the exporting of stability, through military intervention and economic aid, to countries where the state structures have collapsed will succeed in establishing the basic conditions of symmetry, and therefore in guaranteeing a certain reward to state-based political orders.

Statehood linked to a territory, however weak it may be, has the effect that the violation of international rules and international law can be punished in various ways. Networked organizations such as al-Qaeda, on the other hand, cannot be hit with the usual sanctions, and Afghanistan showed that even military strikes of the conventional kind do not completely eliminate the network or permanently impair its ability to function. The strategy of the Europeans in the struggle against international terrorism is to rebuild statehood where it has collapsed in the wake of civil and transnational wars, thereby systematically reducing to a minimum the scope for terrorist networks to sink roots and ensure their survival and operational capability. The Americans are evidently reckoning on a protracted, perhaps permanent, war against terrorist organizations, using short sharp blows to make their offensive capability more and more restricted. But it is more than doubtful whether such a war can ever be won – that is, brought to a successful end. It would be a war on a new 'imperial frontier with the barbarians',[46] which would keep flaring up from time to time.

The European goal of leaving international terrorism high and dry through the rebuilding of statehood does not appear to the Americans to hold much promise of success. This is most clearly expressed in the American use of the term 'rogue states' to describe regimes which covertly support international terrorism as a means of asserting their political will in a situation where they are unable to fight a symmetrical military conflict or (as in the case of Iraq) have already fought and lost one. Rogue states – if the concept is taken seriously – are states that secretly operate with the methods of asymmetrical warfare; they want to cash in twice, to pocket both a symmetry dividend and an asymmetry dividend.

The direction in which this points may be seen from the recent war in Iraq, where the overwhelming military superiority of the United States meant that its by then third-rate enemy was in no position to inflict serious losses on it.[47] The simultaneous conflict with North Korea showed that a threat arising mainly from weapons of mass destruction on the other side clearly limits the American capacity for military action; Pyongyang's statements concerning its nuclear weapons programme were a warning to the United States, and one that Washington took very seriously. The Iraqi regime, however – as the fruitless search by American experts has made apparent – did not have any combat-ready weapons of mass destruction at its disposal. Contrary to official claims, the US administration probably knew that this was the case, or must have assumed it with a high degree of certainty. The asymmetrical superiority of the United States therefore had the effect that the Iraqis stood no chance in classical warfare – and their realization of this is evident from the mass desertions, as well as from the negotiations that top Iraqi officers held over the Internet about the abandonment of all resistance. Things suddenly changed when US and British troops occupied the country and took on the obligation to maintain public order and to ensure the provision of water, fuel and food. As soldiers now had to guard buildings and pipelines, and supplies had to be distributed to troops stationed all over Iraq, military positions and small road convoys became easy targets for underground fighters. It was not long before post-war losses were higher than those sustained in the main period of military confrontation. In a characteristic reversal, whereas asymmetrical force benefited the Americans during the actual war, the post-war situation is being defined by the asymmetrical small war of Iraqi resistance groups.

The latest Gulf war therefore displays the growing asymmetry that is the most important feature of the new wars, and it also shows that the different types of asymmetry do not balance each other out and result in a new symmetry. In symmetrical conflict situations – and this is probably the main reason for the stabilities they generate – the chances for learning and refusal to learn tend to be evenly distributed. Asymmetrical constellations, on the other hand, bring with them inequalities in learning capacity and learning blockage. This suggests that we are heading into extremely turbulent and eventful times.

NOTES

Introduction

1 See Mary Kaldor, *New and Old Wars: Organized Violence in a Global Era* (Cambridge: Polity, 1999).
2 For one determined attempt to abandon the concept of war, at least as a scientific term, see Andreas Osiander, 'Plädoyer für die Abschaffung des "Krieges"', *Initial*, 6 (1995), pp. 23–36.
3 See Herfried Münkler, 'Sind wir im Krieg? Über Terrorismus, Partisanen und die neue Formen des Krieges', *Politische Vierteljahresschrift*, 39, 4 (2001), pp. 581–9.

Chapter 1 What is New about the New Wars?

1 A reliable and informative overview is provided by the annual volumes of the Hamburg-based working group on the causes of war (AKUF). See, most recently, Thomas Rabehl, ed., *Das Kriegsgeschehen 1999: Daten und Tendenzen der Kriege und bewaffneten Konflikte* (Opladen: Hamburger Arbeitsgemeinschaft Kriegsursachenforschung, 2000); and Thomas Rabehl and Wolfgang Schreiber, eds, *Das Kriegsgeschehen 2000: Daten und Tendenzen der Kriege und bewaffneten Konflikte* (Opladen: Hamburger Arbeitsgemeinschaft Kriegsursachenforschung, 2001).
2 See Herfried Münkler, 'Afghanistan: Legitimität der Tradition und Rationalität der Modernisierungs', *Aus Politik und Zeitgeschichte*, 21 (1982), pp. 32–44; and Marin Baraki, 'Die Talibanisierung Afghanistans', *Blätter für deutsche und internationale Politik*, 11 (2001), pp. 1342–52.
3 See Ahmed Rashid, *Taliban: The Story of the Afghan Warlords* (London: Pan Books, 2001), pp. 186–7; and id., *Jihad: The Rise of Militant Islam in Central Asia* (New Haven: Yale University Press, 2002).

4   See Klaus Schlichte and Boris Wilke, 'Der Staat und einige seiner Zeitgenossen: Die Zukunft des Regierens in der "Dritten Welt"', *Zeitschrift für Internationale Beziehungen*, 7, 2 (2000), pp. 359–84, esp. pp. 364ff.

5   This has been argued by, among others, Klaus Jürgen Gantzel, in the debate on the wars following the end of the East–West conflict. See Gantzel, 'Kriegsursachen – Tendenzen und Perspektiven', *Ethik und Sozialwissenschaften: Streitforum für Erwägungskultur*, 8, 3 (1997), pp. 257–66, esp. p. 264. Under the immediate impact of the wars in the former Yugoslavia, Johannes Burkhardt summed up his earlier work in an account of the Thirty Years' War as, in this sense, a state-building war. See his 'Der Dreißigjährige Krieg als frühmoderner Staatsbildungskrieg', *Geschichte in Wissenschaft und Unterricht*, 45 (1984), pp. 487–99.

6   Ryszard Kapuściński, *The Shadow of the Sun: My African Life* (London: Allen Lane, 2001), p. 221.

7   See Wolfgang Reinhard, *Geschichte der Staatsgewalt* (Munich: Beck, 1999), pp. 509ff. For a considerably sharper verdict on the erosion of the state's capacities, see Martin van Creveld, *The Rise and Decline of the State* (Cambridge: Cambridge University Press, 1999), pp. 336ff.

8   Translator's note: See Dietrich Jung, ed., *Shadow Globalization: Ethnic Conflicts and New Wars: A Political Economy of Intra-State War* (London: Routledge, 2003).

9   Edward N. Luttwak, 'Give war a chance', *Foreign Affairs*, 78, 4 (1999), pp. 36–44.

10 David Rieff has shown the disastrous consequences of this embargo policy in the case of the war in Bosnia. See his *Slaughterhouse: Bosnia and the Failure of the West* (New York: Simon & Schuster, 1995), especially on the embargo policy and the calculations underlying it (pp. 27ff.).

11 See the figures in Wolfgang Schreiber, 'Die Kriege in der zweiten Hälfte des 20. Jahrhunderts und danach', in Rabehl and Schreiber, *Das Kriegsgeschehen 2000*, pp. 16–17.

12 Carl von Clausewitz, *On War*, ed. Anatol Rapoport (Harmondsworth: Penguin Books, 1968), pp. 330, 337 (Book IV, chapters 9 and 10).

13 If a decision to the war was sought in a great battle, this obviously does not mean that it was found there. Either the enemy might avoid contact, preferring to have the decisive encounter at a different time and place, or the battle might not bring a decision because neither side emerged as clear victor, or the victor might be too exhausted to exploit his victory. But this does not alter the fact that most European inter-state wars were decided by a great battle. In their case – and usually only in their case – a history of war as essentially a history of great battles is appropriate. Cf. Stig Förster, Markus Pöhlmann and Dierk Walter, eds, *Schlachten der Weltgeschichte* (Munich: Beck, 2001).

14 See Peter M. Kuhfus, 'Die Anfänge der Volkskriegsdoktrin in China', in Gerhard Schulz, ed., *Partisanen und Volkskrieg: Zur Revolutionierung*

des Krieges im 20. Jahrhundert (Göttingen: Vandenhoeck & Ruprecht, 1985), pp. 57–91, esp. pp. 64ff. In both wars in Vietnam, first against France and then against the Saigon regime and the United States, General Giap applied Mao's three-stage doctrine of moving from strategic defensive through strategic equilibrium to strategic offensive. The first war ended with the French defeat at Dien Bien Phu, and the second with the capture of Saigon by regular North Vietnamese troops.

15 See Martin van Creveld, *On Future War* (London: Brassey's, 1991), pp. 18ff.

16 Vesna Bojicic, Mary Kaldor and Ivan Vejvoda, *Post-War Reconstruction in the Balkans: A Background Report Prepared for the European Commission*, Sussex European Institute Working Paper No. 14 (Brighton: 1995), p. 39.

17 Hugo Grotius, *De iure belli ac pacis* (Tübingen: 1950).

18 These percentages are naturally based on estimates rather than precise counts, and there are also problems of definition and categorization. For the early twentieth century, see Dan Smith, *The State of War and Peace Atlas* (Oslo: International Peace Research Institute, 1997); and for the turn of the twentieth century Mary Kaldor, *New and Old Wars: Organized Violence in a Global Era* (Cambridge: Polity, 1999), p. 100. See also Klaus Jürgen Gantzel, 'Über die Kriege nach dem Zweiten Weltkrieg: Tendenzen, ursächliche Hintergründe, Perspektiven', in Bernd Wegner, ed., *Wie Kriege entstehen: Zum historischen Hintergrund von Staatenkonflikten* (Paderborn: Schöningh, 2000), pp. 299–318, esp. pp. 308ff.

19 Cf. François Jean and Jean-Christophe Rufin, eds, *Économie des guerres civiles* (Paris: Hachette, 1996); and Mats Berdal and David D. Malone, eds, *Greed and Grievance: Economic Agendas in Civil Wars* (Boulder, Colo.: Lynne Rienner Publishers, 2000).

20 See Philipp Genschel and Klaus Schlichte, 'Wenn Kriege chronisch werden: Der Bürgerkrieg', *Leviathan*, 25, 4 (1997), pp. 501–17, esp. pp. 507ff.

21 The best analyses of massacre as the practice of violence may be found in Wolfgang Sofsky, *Traktat über die Gewalt* (Frankfurt am Main: S. Fischer, 1996), pp. 173ff.; and id., *Violence, Terrorism, Genocide, War* (London: Granta Books, 2003), pp. 162–7.

22 For an initial survey of these phenomena, see Gaby Zipfel, ' "Blood, sperm and tears": Sexuelle Gewalt in Kriegen', *Mittelweg 36*, 10, 5 (2001), pp. 3–20 (translated online as ' "Blood, sperm and tears": Sexual violence in war', http://www.eurozine.com/article/2001-11-29-zipfel-en.html); and Kevin Gerard Neill, 'Duty, honor, rape: Sexual assault against women during war', *Journal of International Women's Studies*, 2, 1 (2001).

23 Hans Christoph Buch, *Blut im Schuh: Schlächter und Voyeure an den Fronten des Weltbürgerkriegs* (Frankfurt am Main: Eichborn, 2001), p. 117. On the connection between the displaying of human body parts as trophies and the collapse of traditional religious interpretations of the world, see Stephen Ellis (also writing on the Liberian civil war), *The Mask of Anarchy* (London: Hurst, 1999).

24 In the late Middle Ages and the early modern period, the Four Horsemen of the Apocalypse depicted in John's *Book of Revelation* (6: 1–8) were decoded as pestilence, soaring prices, war and death.

25 One expression of this is the famous declaration by the Berlin City Commandant after the Prussian defeat at Jena and Auerstedt: 'The King has lost a battle. Now calm is the citizen's first duty!' (quoted from Thomas Nipperdey, *Deutsche Geschichte 1800–1866: Bürgerwelt und starker Staat* (Munich: Beck, 1983), p. 15). War was only remotely connected with people's daily lives and was not expected to lead to social catastrophes. Thus, from the end of the Thirty Years' War to the beginning of the First World War, the wars fought in Europe had only a minor impact on demographic trends. (Of course, this was not true of the European wars of conquest in other continents.) With regard to the wars of the sixteenth to eighteenth centuries, the difficulties and cost of regularly feeding the troops and staving off epidemics may be gauged from the average causes of death: only one in ten soldiers who lost their lives during a war actually fell on the battlefield; three in ten died as a result of their wounds; and six in ten succumbed to inadequate nourishment and the resulting deficiency disorders or infections. See Bernhard R. Kroener, ' "Das Schwungrad der Staatsmaschine"? Die Beudeutung der bewaffneten Macht in der europäischen Geschichte der Frühen Neuzeit', in Bernard Kroener and Ralf Pröve, eds, *Krieg und Frieden: Militär und Gesellschaft in der Frühen Neuzeit* (Paderborn: Schöningh, 1996), pp. 1–23, here p. 11.

26 For an initial survey, see Berndt Georg Thamm, 'The nexus between arms trade, drugs and terrorism', in Alex P. Schmidt, ed., *Countering Terrorism through International Cooperation* (Milan: UN Terrorism Prevention Branch, 2001), pp. 109–18.

27 The political and economic line-ups in Colombia are marked by an antagonistic coalition of guerrilla groups, military forces and organized crime. The term 'antagonistic coalition' means that all three players fight against one another but also indirectly cooperate, because they derive considerable benefits from the status quo that would be lost if the civil war were to end. In his 'The political economy of violence: The war system in Colombia' (*Journal of Interamerican Studies and World Affairs*, 39, 2 (1997), pp. 37–82), Nazih Richani concludes that there are direct economic links among guerrillas, drug dealers, army officers, paramilitary groups and private security firms.

28 On the tacit coalition between Russian soldiers and Chechen fighters in the first Chechen war of the mid-1990s, see Juan Goytisolo, *Landscapes of War* (San Francisco: City Lights Books, 2000). And on kidnapping and the trade in dead bodies as means of personal enrichment by officers and soldiers of the Russian army in the second Chechen war, see Anne Nivat, *Chienne de Guerre: A Woman Reporter behind the Lines of the War in Chechnya* (New York: Public Affairs, 2001).

29 Rieff, *Slaughterhouse*, p. 88.

30 See Mark Duffield, 'Post-modern conflict: Warlords, post-adjustment states and private protection', *Civil Wars*, 1, 1 (1998), pp. 65–102; and Herfried Münkler, 'Die privatisierten Kriege des 21. Jahrhunderts', *Merkur*, 55, 3 (2001), pp. 222–34.

31 For an excellent overview of the history and contemporary reality of warlord configurations, see Michael Riekenberg, 'Warlords: Eine Problemskizze', *Comparativ*, 5–6 (1999), pp. 187–205; also William Reno, *Warlord Politics and African States* (Boulder, Colo.: Lynne Rienner Publishers, 1998). On the first modern instance of warlord rule, in China in the 1920s, 1930s and 1940s, see Edward A. McCord, *The Power of the Gun: The Emergence of Modern Chinese Warlordism* (Berkeley: University of California Press, 1993). And on other profiteers from the de-statization of war, see Klaus Schichte, 'Profiteure und Verlierer von Bürgerkriegsökonomien', text of a presentation given at the Economics of Civil Wars conference, Hofgeismar, 19–21 October 2001.

32 Riekenberg, 'Warlords', p. 200.

33 Hartmut Diessenbacher, *Kriege der Zukunft: Die Bevölkerungsexplosion gefährdet den Frieden* (Munich: Hanser, 1998), esp. pp. 185ff.

34 Kapuściński, *The Shadow of the Sun*, p. 255.

35 Cf. François Jean, 'Aide humanitaire et économie de guerre', in Jean and Rufin, *Économie*, pp. 543–89. An exemplary study of the use of humanitarian aid by participants in the Liberian civil war may be found in Fabrice Weissman, *L'Aide humanitaire dans la dynamique du conflict libérien* (Paris: Fondation Médecins sans Frontières, 1996). Another case in point is the siege and bombardment of Sarajevo in 1992–6, when Bosnian Serb forces allowed UN relief convoys to pass through only if they were first able to help themselves to the supplies.

36 Pino Arlacchi, *Ware Mensch: Der Skandal des modernen Sklavenhandels* (Munich: Piper, 1999), p. 164. Original: *Schiavi: il nuovo traffico di esseri umani* (Milan: Rizzoli, 1999).

37 Kapuściński, *The Shadow of the Sun*, pp. 148–9. Significantly, after the East–West conflict ended and major powers became less interested in the arming of political allies, arms sales to the African continent declined from $5.2 billion to $500 million. This was reflected in a switch from heavy weapons such as tanks and fighter aircraft to weapons such as rifles, machine-guns, landmines and light artillery, which are the ones mainly used in the new wars.

38 Peter Scholl-Latour, *Afrikanische Totenklage: Der Ausverkauf des Schwarzen Kontinents* (Munich: Bertelsmann, 2001), p. 439.

39 Buch, *Blut im Schuh*, p. 31.

40 Michael Ignatieff, *The Warrior's Honour: Ethnic War and the Modern Conscience* (London: Chatto & Windus, 1998), pp. 127–8.

41 Clotilde Twagiramariya and Meredeth Turshen, ' "Favors" to give and "consenting" victims: The sexual politics of survival in Rwanda', in *What Women Do in Wartime: Gender and Conflict in Africa* (London: Zed Books, 1998), p. 102. Gourevitch also reports systematic rapes

accompanying the massacre of Tutsis: see Philip Gourevitch, *We wish to inform you that tomorrow we will be killed with our families: Stories from Rwanda* (New York: Farrar, Straus & Giroux, 1998).

42   Instead of relating it to the breakdown of discipline among the armed groups, much of the specialist literature on war rape treats it as a constant phenomenon in any kind of war. It thus largely escapes most authors that the incidence of rape dramatically increased in the transition from inter-state wars (where it was a crime that could be judged before a court martial) to the new wars (where it has become an element of war strategy).

43   See Duffield, 'Post-modern conflict', pp. 92ff.

44   Scholl-Latour, *Afrikanische Totenklage*, p. 430.

45   Ibid.

46   This found expression in the concept of a new world order, entertained by George Bush, Sr and by François Mitterrand.

47   The relevant figures may be found in Gantzel, 'Über die Kriege nach dem Zweiten Weltkrieg', pp. 300ff.

48   The idea of a global civil law may be found in Jürgen Habermas, 'Bestialität und Humanität: Ein Krieg an der Grenze zwischen Recht und Moral', in Reinhard Merkel, ed., *Der Kosovo-Krieg und das Völkerrecht* (Frankfurt am Main: Suhrkamp, 2000), pp. 51–65 (translated online as 'Bestiality and humanity: A war on the border between law and morality', http://www.theglobalsite.ac.uk/press/011habermas.htm). The theorem of democratic peace rests upon the observation that democracies never or almost never wage war against democracies – although it should also be noted that democracies often wage war against countries with other systems of rule. Does this mean that perpetual peace could be achieved if all countries were democracies? What this debate nearly always overlooks is that the theorem of democratic peace refers to inter-state wars, which are themselves tending to disappear. It has nothing to say about the intra-state and transnational wars that have been the most prevalent form in the past ten to twenty years.

49   On the formulation of the concept and the development of a theoretical model, see Peter Waldmann, 'Bürgerkrieg – Annäherung an einen schwer fassbaren Begriff', *Leviathan*, 25, 4 (1997), pp. 480–500, and Genschel and Schlichte, 'Wenn Kriege chronisch werden'. A set of case studies on the application of the concept may be found in Heinrich-W. Krumwiede and Peter Waldmann, eds, *Bürgerkriege: Folgen und Regulierungsmöglichkeiten* (Baden-Baden: Nomos Verlag, 1998). Hans Magnus Enzensberger offers an exaggerated application of the civil war concept in his *Aussichten auf den Bürgerkrieg* (Frankfurt am Main: Suhrkamp, 1993). See also Roman Schnur, 'Zwischenbilanz: Zur Theorie des Bürgerkriegs. Bemerkungen über einen vernachlässigten Gegenstand', *Revolution und Weltbürgerkrieg: Studien zur Ouverture nach 1789* (Berlin: Duncker & Humblot, 1983), pp. 120–45.

50 This idea is most succinctly presented in Christopher Daase, *Kleine Kriege – Große Wirkung: Wie unkonventionelle Kriegsführung die internationale Politik verändert* (Baden-Baden: Nomos Verlag, 1999), esp. pp. 213ff. Cf. the discussion with Martin Hoch in *Mittelweg 36*, 10, 1 (2001), pp. 45–9; and Martin Hoch, 'Krieg und Politik im 21. Jahrhundert', *Aus Politik und Zeitgeschichte*, 20 (2001), pp. 17–25.

51 See Johannes Kunisch, *Der Kleine Krieg: Studien zum Heerwesen des Absolutismus*, Frankfurter Historische Abhandlungen, vol. 4 (Wiesbaden: Steiner, 1973), esp. pp. 5–24.

52 This idea is less marked but certainly present in the Castro–Guevara doctrine of guerrilla warfare, and it is central to Mao Zedong's guerrilla strategy and its various derivatives (see his *Theorie des Guerrillakrieges oder Strategie der Dritten Welt* (Reinbek: Rowohlt, 1966)), as well as to Tito's conception of partisan warfare that became the accepted thing in south-east Europe (see Milovan Djilas, *Wartime* (London: Martin Secker & Warburg, 1977), pp. 201ff.).

53 Sofsky, *Violence, Terrorism, Genocide, War*, pp. 151–90.

54 Enzensberger, *Aussichten auf den Bürgerkrieg*, pp. 18ff.

55 Trutz von Trotha, 'Formen des Krieges: Zur Typologie kriegerischer Aktionsmacht', in Sighard Neckel and Michael Schwab-Trapp, eds, *Ordnungen der Gewalt: Beiträge zu einer politischen Soziologie der Gewalt und des Krieges* (Opladen: Leske und Budrich, 1999), pp. 71–95, here pp. 87ff.

56 Lack of empirical knowledge is another factor, as good descriptive accounts of the new wars are few and far between. We are forced to rely overwhelmingly on the reports of journalists – that is to say, war correspondents.

57 As far as I am aware, Mary Kaldor was the first to use the term 'new wars': see her *New and Old Wars*.

58 The conflict between Israel and the Palestinian authority represents in miniature a regionally limited copy of the global political line-ups: on the one side, the most powerful military apparatus in the region; on the other side, a political structure which claims for itself the character of a state and which has no heavy weapons of its own, not to speak of an air force. On the so-called first intifada of the late 1980s, see John Bunzl and Nadia El-Masri, eds, *Der Aufstand: Palästinensische und israelische Stimmen zur Intifada* (Vienna: Passagen-Verlag, 1989).

59 Rieff, *Slaughterhouse*, p. 160.

60 Quoted (and retranslated) from Michael Birnbaum, *Krisenherd Somalia: Das Land des Terrors und der Anarchie* (Munich: Heyne, 2002), p. 15. See also Peter Bergen, *Heiliger Krieg, Inc: Osama Bin Ladens Terrornetz* (Berlin: Berliner Taschenbuch-Verlag, 2001), pp. 151ff.

61 For greater detail on these points, see Peter Waldmann, *Terrorismus: Provokation der Macht* (Munich: Gerling Akademie Verlag, 1998); and Herfried Münkler, 'Terrorismus als Kommunikationsstrategie: Die Botschaft des 11. September', *Internationale Politik*, 56, 12 (2001), pp. 11–18.

62   See Raymond Aron, *Peace and War: A Theory of International Relations* (London: Weidenfeld & Nicolson, 1962), pp. 33–4.

63   Cf. Götz Neuneck, 'Virtuelle Rüstungen: Die Waffensysteme des 21. Jahrhunderts oder die USA rüsten mit sich selbst', in *Wissenschaft und Frieden*, W & F Dossier No. 31 (Marburg: BdWi Verlag, 1999), pp. 10–15; and Ulrich Albrecht, 'Neue Technologien der Kriegsführung und ihre Auswirkungen auf die internationale Ordnung', *Politik und Technik*, special issue no. 31, *Politische Vierteljahresschrift* (2000), pp. 293–301; both, of course, without referring to the new asymmetries and therefore with an accusatory attitude towards the United States.

64   On the beginnings of this development in Vitoria, Ayala, Gentili, Suárez and Grotius, see Wilhelm Grewe, *The Epochs of International Law* (Berlin/New York: de Gruyter, 2000).

65   Carl Schmitt repeatedly pointed to this aspect in his use of the concept of 'undiscriminating war between states'. See his *Der Nomos der Erde im Völkerrecht des Jus Publicum Europaeum* (Cologne: Greven, 1950), pp. 123–43.

66   On the asymmetrical legitimation of war by Islamic fundamentalism, see Gilles Kepel, *Jihad: The Trail of Political Islam* (London: I. B. Tauris, 2003), *passim*. On Western intellectuals and the the idea of just war, mainly with reference to arguments centred on human rights, see David Luban, 'Just war and human rights', in Charles R. Beitz et al., eds, *International Ethics* (Princeton, NJ: Princeton University Press, 1985), pp. 195–216.

Chapter 2   Warfare, State Building and the Thirty Years' War

1   Trutz von Trotha, 'Die Zukunft liegt in Afrika: Vom Zerfall des Staates, von der Vorherrschaft der konzentrischen Ordnung und vom Aufstieg der Parastaatlichkeit', *Leviathan*, 28, 2 (2000), pp. 253–79; and id., 'Über den Erfolg und die Brüchigkeit der Utopie staatlicher Herrschaft: Herrschaftssoziologische Betrachtungen über den kolonialen und nachkolonialen Staat in Westafrika', in Wolfgang Reinhard, ed., *Verstaatlichung der Welt? Europäische Staatsmodelle und außereuropäische Machtprozesse* (Munich: Oldenbourg, 1999), pp. 223–51.

2   Martin van Creveld, *On Future War* (London: Brassey's, 1991), pp. 57ff., 171ff., 207f.; and id., *The Rise and Decline of the State* (Cambridge: Cambridge University Press, 1999), pp. 337ff.

3   Of course, Clausewitz himself was not always of this view. Under the immediate impact of the Napoleonic wars, he too at least metaphorically attributed to war the role of a subject in its own right. See the chapter on Clausewitz's instrumental and existential conceptions of war, in my *Über den Krieg: Stationen der Kriegsgeschichte im Spiegel ihrer theoretischen Reflexion* (Weilerwist: Velbrück, 2002), pp. 91–115.

4   Carl von Clausewitz, *On War*, ed. Anatol Rapoport (Harmondsworth: Penguin Books, 1968), p. 367 (Book V, chapter 2).
5   Ibid., p. 402 (Book V, chapter 6). It is another matter whether Clausewitz's points were altogether empirically accurate, and doubts have been continually raised about this. See, among others, Klaus Jürgen Gantzel, 'Tolstoi statt Clausewitz? Überlegungen zum Verhältnis von Staat und Krieg seit 1816 mittels statistischer Beobachtungen', in Reiner Steinweg, ed., *Kriegsursachen*, Friedensanalysen No. 21 (Frankfurt am Main: Suhrkamp, 1987), pp. 25–97.
6   Immanuel Kant, with the French Revolution in mind, spoke of a historical sign in which he could recognize a moral tendency in human history. In the present case, the indications would seem to point to an opposite tendency.
7   See, for example, Ekkehart Krippendorff, *Staat und Krieg: Die historische Logik politischer Unvernunft* (Frankfurt am Main: Suhrkamp, 1985); and my critical comments on this work in 'Staat, Krieg und Frieden: Die verwechselte Wechselsbeziehung', in Steinweg, *Kriegsursachen*, pp. 135–44.
8   Christopher Daase has examined in detail the profound consequences of this trend. In his view, large wars tend to stabilize the international order, whereas small wars have brought about its gradual erosion. See Christopher Daase, *Kleine Kriege – Grosse Wirkung: Wie unkonventielle Kriegführung die internationale Politik verändert* (Baden-Baden: Nomos Verlag, 1999), esp. pp. 91ff.
9   Barbara Ehrenreich, for instance, conceives of war as a 'self-reproducing pattern of behaviour': see her *Blood Rites: Origins and History of the Passions of War* (London: Virago, 1997). More subtle in their treatment are Cora Stephan, *Das Handwerk des Krieges* (Berlin: Rowohlt Berlin, 1998) and John Keegan, *A History of Warfare* (London: Hutchinson, 1993).
10 Critical on this point is Andreas Herberg-Rothe, 'Clausewitz oder Nietzsche: Zum Paradigmenwechsel in der politischen Theorie des Krieges', *Merkur 623*, 55, 3 (2001), pp. 246–50.
11 See my essay 'Bleiben die Staaten die Herren des Krieges?', in Karl Graf Ballestrem, Volker Gerhardt, Henning Ottmann and Martyn P. Thompson, eds, *Politisches Denken: Jahrbuch 2000* (Stuttgart-Weimar: Metzler, 2000), pp. 16–34.
12 Boris Cezarevic Urlanis, *Bilanz der Kriege: Die Menschenverluste Europas vom 17. Jahrhundert bis zur Gegenwart* (Berlin: Deutscher Verlag der Wissenschaften, 1965).
13 The best and most exhaustive account of medieval warfare is still Philippe Contamine, *War in the Middle Ages* (Oxford: Blackwell, 1984).
14 Clausewitz, *On War*, pp. 343–4 (Book IV, chapter 11).
15 Jürgen Osterhammel, 'Kulturelle Grenzen in der Expansion Europas', *Saeculum*, 46, 1 (1995), pp. 101–38, here p. 109.
16 This is not the same as Carl Schmitt's celebrated idea that the distinctively political decision is the one that identifies friend and enemy; see

Carl Schmitt, *The Concept of the Political* (New Brunswick, NJ: Rutgers University Press, 1976), pp. 26–7. Whereas Schmitt claims to define the constitutive criterion of the political, my point here is that the state as such claims a monopoly on the differentiation between friend and enemy, and at least in the event of war makes its decision binding on its citizens.

17 See my discussion of the example of Connetable de Bourbon in Herfried Münkler, *Im Namen des Staates: Die Staatsraison in der Frühen Neuzeit* (Frankfurt am Main: S. Fischer, 1987), pp. 209–10.

18 For a more detailed discussion, see Johannes Kunisch, *Der Kleine Krieg: Studien zum Heerwesen des Absolutismus*, Frankfurter Historische Abhandlungen, vol. 4 (Wiesbaden: Steiner, 1973), pp. 5–24.

19 On the disciplining effects of the quartering of troops in barracks, see Ralf Pröve, 'Der Soldat in der "guten Bürgerstube": Das frühneuzeitliche Einquartierungssystem und die sozioökonomischen Folgen', in Bernhard Kroener and Ralf Pröve, eds, *Krieg und Frieden: Militär und Gesellschaft in der Frühen Neuzeit* (Paderborn: Schöningh, 1966), pp. 191–217. And on the replacement of peer-group courts with a courts-martial system, see Peter Burschel, 'Zur Sozialgeschichte innermilitärischer Disziplinierung im 16. und 17. Jahrhundert', *Zeitschrift für Geschichtswissenschaft*, 42, 11 (1994), pp. 965–81, here pp. 971–2.

20 On the roving landsknechts and their hangers-on, see Reinhard Baumann, *Landsknechte: Ihre Geschichte und Kultur vom späten Mittelalter bis zum Dreißigjährigen Krieg* (Munich: Beck, 1994), pp. 131ff.; and Burschel, 'Zur Sozialgeschichte innermilitärischer Disziplinierung', pp. 977ff.

21 On these conventions, see Jost Dülffer, 'Regeln im Krieg? Kriegsverbrechen und die Haager Friedenskonferenz', in Wolfram Wette and Gerd R. Ueberschär, eds, *Kriegsverbrechen im 20. Jahrhundert* (Darmstadt: Wissenschaftliche Buchgesellschaft, 2001), pp. 35–49.

22 Wette and Ueberschär, *Kriegsverbrechen*, contains many detailed studies in this connection.

23 This trend is documented in Roy Gutmann and David Rieff, eds, *Crimes of War: What the Public Should Know* (New York: W.W. Norton & Co., 1999).

24 On the concept of a 'violence market', see Georg Elwert, 'Gewaltmärkte: Beobachtungen zur Zweckrationalität der Gewalt', in Trutz von Trotha, ed., *Soziologie der Gewalt*, Special issue no. 37 of the *Kölner Zeitschrift für Soziologie und Sozialpsychologie* (Opladen: Westdeutscher Verlag, 1997), pp. 86–101.

25 See Bernhard R. Kroener, 'Vom "extraordinari Kriegsvolck" zum "miles perpetuus": Zur Rolle der bewaffneten Macht in der europäischen Gesellschaft der frühen Neuzeit', *Militärgeschichtliche Mitteilungen*, 43, 1 (1988), pp. 141–87; Martin C. Mandlmayr and Karl G. Vocelka, 'Vom Adelsaufgebot zum stehenden Heer: Bemerkungen zum Funktionswandel des Adels im Kriegwesen der frühen Neuzeit', *Wiener Beiträge*

zur Geschichte der Neuzeit, 8 (1982), pp. 112–25; Rainer Wohlfeil, 'Das Heerwesen im Übergang vom Ritter- zum Söldnerheer', in Johannes Kunisch, ed., *Staatsverfassung und Heeresverfassung in der europäischen Geschichte der frühen Neuzeit*, in collaboration with Barbara Stollberg-Rillinger (Berlin: Duncker & Humblot, 1986), pp. 107–27; and Hans Schmidt, 'Staat und Armee im Zeitalter des "miles perpetuus" ', in Kunisch, *Staatsverfassung und Heeresverfassung*, pp. 213–48.

26   One expression of this was the fact that scarcely any short-term service contracts were signed from now on, as the various states strove to tie in the soldiery for long periods of time.

27   See Burschel, 'Zur Sozialgeschichte innermilitärischer Disziplinierung', pp. 975ff.

28   In the case of Germany, Peter Englund concludes: 'The war strengthened and deepened a certain economic stagnation which had already begun before its outbreak. The great prosperity of the sixteenth century was all but exhausted after the thirty years of war. Many towns and communities which had enjoyed large surpluses before 1618 were deep in debt after 1648, having been repeatedly forced to make financial contributions and to pay various sums under the threat of pillaging and burning. In addition, there were the five million thalers that Swedish diplomats extorted from the Reich as their price for agreeing to peace, which in many cases swallowed up the little capital still available. The interest alone on the huge loans would weigh on people for generations.' (Peter Englund, *Die Verwüstung Deutschlands: Eine Geschichte des Dreißigjährigen Krieges* (Stuttgart: Klett-Cotta, 1998), p. 590.) Christopher Friedrichs is considerably more cautious in his judgement of the long-term consequences: see his 'The war and German society', in Geoffrey Parker, *The Thirty Years' War* (London: Routledge & Kegan Paul, 1984), pp. 208–15.

29   This phenomenon, known in German history as *Brandschatzung*, involved the marching of troops up to the walls of a city and the extraction of money through threats of pillage and burning. It was thus a hybrid of ransom and a form of plunder limited by formal agreement.

30   For further description and analysis of the war, see Parker, *The Thirty Years' War* and Herbert Langer, *The Thirty Years' War* (Poole: Blandford, 1980). A rich compilation of eye-witness reports and documents as well as contemporary pictures may be found in Peter Milger, *Gegen Land und Leute: Der Dreißigjährige Krieg* (Munich: Bertelsmann, 1998). Whereas Milger focuses mainly on violence against the civilian population, Englund's *Die Verwüstung Deutschlands* contains the most vivid and accurate accounts from the second half of the war that I have come across in the literature. On the life of the soldiers, see especially Bernhard R. Kroener, ' "Kriegsgurgeln, Freireuter und Merodebrüder": Der Soldat des Dreißigjährigen Krieges. Täter und Opfer', in Wolfram Wette, ed., *Der Krieg des kleinen Mannes: Eine Militärgeschichte von unten* (Munich: Piper, 1992), pp. 51–67.

31   A not insignificant part of these troops consisted of former mercenaries of the fallen warlord who were taken into the service of the one who appeared in his place. Moreover, many a captured mercenary would switch sides without further ado and fight in the ranks of the former enemy. After the capitulation of Rothenburg ob der Tauber, 500 men from the 800-strong imperial garrison threw in their lot with the Swedes. This caused a great sensation, especially as the imperial forces had been assured free passage out of the town 'with flags flying and fuses burning, with bag and baggage'. See Milger, *Gegen Land und Leute*, p. 254.

32   The figure is taken from Langer, *The Thirty Years' War*, p. 8.

33   Quoted from Milger, *Gegen Land und Leute*, p. 137.

34   Bernhard Kroener has considerably qualified and circumscribed the picture of a complete breakdown of order and discipline during the Thirty Years' War: see his 'Soldat oder Soldateska? Programmatischer Aufriss einer Sozialgeschichte militärischer Unterschichten in der ersten Hälfte des 17. Jahrhunderts', in Manfred Messerschmidt et al., eds, *Militärgeschichte: Probleme, Thesen, Wege* (Stuttgart: Deutsche Verlags-Anstalt, 1982), pp. 100–23. Cf. id., ' "Die Soldaten sind ganz arm, bloss, nackend, ausgemattet": Lebensverhältnisse und Organisationsstruktur der militärischen Gesellschaft während des Dreißigjährigen Krieges', in Klaus Bußmann and Heinz Schilling, eds, *1648: Krieg und Frieden in Europa* (Münster: Westfälisches Landesmuseum für Kunst und Kulturgeschichte, 1998), pp. 285–92.

35   Quoted from Milger, *Gegen Land und Leute*, p. 212.

36   In its German etymological life, the term *marodieren* ('to maraud') derives from the adjective *marode*, which in soldiers' language meant 'incapable of marching' or 'road-weary'. *Marodeure* or *Marodebrüder* ('marauders') were thus originally stragglers who were cut off from the military supply system and had to find their own shelter and provisions. The term then soon came to denote plundering soldiers on the margins of the main army. Such forms of self-provision were part and parcel of the war conducted by *Parteigänger* (originally, partisans in the sense of members of a party), which later came to be known as *Partisanenkrieg* (partisan warfare).

37   See Langer, *The Thirty Years' War*, pp. 103ff., esp. p. 107.

38   Johann Jakob Grimmelshausen, *Simplicissimus*, trans. S. Goodrich (Sawtry: Dedalus, 1989).

39   Johann Michael Moscherosch, *Geschichte Philanders von Sittewald* (Darmstadt: Wissenschaftliche Buchgesellschaft, 1964).

40   *Simplicissimus* should not, of course, be read as a historical source, as it often is. In fact, Grimmelshausen's own fifteen years of military service enter only marginally into his book: see Dieter Breuer, 'Krieg und Frieden in Grimmelshausens *Simplicissimus Deutsch*', *Der Deutschunterricht*, 37, 5 (1985), pp. 79–101.

41   See Wolfgang Reinhard, *Geschichte der Staatsgewalt* (Munich: Beck, 1999), p. 347. On the type and activity of the war entrepreneur, a

key reference is still Fritz Redlich, *The German Military Enterpriser and His Work Force*, issues 47 and 48 of *Vierteljahresschrift für Sozial- und Wirtschaftsgeschichte* (Wiesbaden: 1964/5). For a concise survey of the funding and organization of the troops, see Herbert Langer, 'Heeresfinanzierung, Produktion und Märkte für die Kriegführung', in Bußmann and Schilling, *1648*, pp. 293–9.

42   On Piccolomini and Lobkowitz, see Thomas M. Barker, *Army, Aristocracy, Monarchy: Essays on War, Society and Government in Austria, 1618–1780* (Boulder: Colo.: Social Science Monographs, 1982), pp. 61ff and 112ff. On the new type of social careers in general, see Rainer Wohlfeil, 'Ritter – Söldnerführer – Offizier': Versuch eines vergleichs', in Arno Borst, ed., *Das Rittertum im Mittelalter* (Darmstadt: Wissenschaftliche Buchgesellschaft, 1976), pp. 315–48, esp. pp. 329ff.

43   Konrad Repgen provides a succinct overview in 'Die westfälischen Friedensverhandlungen: Überblick und Hauptprobleme', in Bußmann and Schilling, *1648*, pp. 355–72.

44   See, for example, *1648/1998: Frieden als Aufgabe*, evening public lectures delivered at the Münster historians' conference between 27 October and 12 November 1996 (Lengerich: 1996).

45   Thucydides should be seen as the 'inventor' of this way of seeing things. His *History of the Peloponnesian War* also combined and 'wrote together' (*xyngraphé*) several partly sequential, partly overlapping wars.

46   Christine Noelle-Karimi, Conrad Schetter and Reinhard Schlagintweit, eds, *Afghanistan – A Country without a State?* (Frankfurt am Main: Verlag für Interkulturelle Kommunikation, 2002). On the course of the conflict over the past ten years, see Ahmed Rashid, *Taliban: The Story of the Afghan Warlords* (London: Pan Books, 2001).

47   See Victoria Brittain, *Death of Dignity: Angola's Civil War* (London: Pluto Press, 1998).

48   See Bartholomäus Grill, 'Der afrikanische Weltkrieg', *Die Zeit*, 22 February 2001, p. 3.

49   See Ludwig Watzal, *Feinde des Friedens: Der endlose Konflikt zwischen Israel und den Palästinensern* (Berlin: Aufbau, 2001); and William Harris, *Faces of Lebanon: Sects, Wars, and Global Extension* (Princeton, NJ: Markus Wiener, 1997).

50   In the case of *transnationalization* – which it is important to distinguish from *internationalization*, at least analytically – not states but infra-state players cross the boundaries of a conflict that is intra-state to the extent that it is conducted on the territory of a (former) state. Of course, this distinction cannot always be clearly made, but it is evident that, precisely in this context, the privatization of war and the limits set to it are factors of central importance.

51   This interpretation may be found especially in the work of Carl Schmitt and his school, in conjunction with a view grounded in political theory according to which there are parallels between the ideological conflicts of the twentieth century and the religious wars of the sixteenth

and seventeenth centuries. See, for example, Roman Schnur, *Die Rolle der Juristen bei der Entstehung des modernen Staates* (Berlin: Duncker & Humblot, 1962); id., *Revolution und Weltbürgerkrieg: Studien zur Ouverture nach 1789* (Berlin: Duncker & Humblot, 1983); and Hanno Kesting, *Geschichtsphilosophie und Weltbürgerkrieg: Deutungen der Geschichte von der Französischen Revolution bis zum Ost-West-Konflikt* (Heidelberg: Winter, 1959).

52   See Johannes Burkhardt, 'Worum ging es im Dreißigjährigen Krieg? Die frühmodernen Koflikte um Konfessions- und Staatsbildung', in Bernd Wegner, ed., *Wie Kriege entstehen: Zum historischen Hintergrund von Staatenkonflikten*, vol. 4: *Kriege in der Geschichte* (Paderborn: Schöningh, 2000), pp. 67–87.

53   On the Swedish king, see Günter Barudio, *Gustav Adolf – der Große: Eine politische Biographie* (Frankfurt am Main: S. Fischer, 1982).

54   See especially Jörg Wollenberg, *Richelieu: Staatsräson und Kircheninteresse: Zur Legitimation der Politik des Kardinalpremier* (Bielefeld: Pfeffer, 1977), pp. 39–124.

55   See Redlich, *The German Military Enterpriser*.

56   On the great significance of the Renaissance goddess Fortuna for freewheeling mercenaries, see Langer, *The Thirty Years' War*, pp. 61, 94, 158, 201. Anton Ernstberger provides insight into their imaginative world in his *Abenteurer des Dreißigjährigen Krieges: Zur Kulturgeschichte der Zeit* (Erlangen: Universitätsbibliothek, 1963), which includes an analysis and evaluation of the correspondence between two sons of a Nuremberg patrician who became soldiers to make their fortune at war.

Chapter 3   The Statization of War

1   The incident was recorded and handed down in Franco Sacchetti's Novella CLXXXI (*Il Trecentonovelle*, online at http://www.liberliber.it/biblioteca/s/sacchetti); cf. Franco Sacchetti, *Die wandernden Leuchtkäfer: Renaissancenovellen aus der Toskana* (Berlin: Wagenbach, 1991), part two, pp. 80–1.

2   See Michael Howard, *War in European History* (London: Oxford University Press, 1976), pp. 33–55; Michael E. Mallett, *Mercenaries and their Masters: Warfare in Renaissance Italy* (London: Bodley Head, 1974); and John R. Hale, *War and Society in Renaissance Europe, 1450–1620* (Stroud: Sutton, 1998), pp. 127ff. See also the keyword 'Condottieri' in Herfried and Marina Münkler, *Lexikon der Renaissance* (Munich: Beck, 2000), pp. 57–67.

3   See Hans Michael Möller, *Das Regiment der Landsknechte: Untersuchungen zu Verfassung, Recht und Selbstverständnis in deutschen Söldnerheeren des 16. Jahrhunderts*, Frankfurter historische Abhandlungen, vol. 12 (Wiesbaden: Steiner, 1976); Reinhard Baumann, *Landsknechte: Ihre Geschichte und Kultur vom späten Mittelalter bis zum Dreißigjährigen*

Krieg (Munich: Beck, 1994); cf. the older account in Friedrich Blau, *Die deutschen Landsknechte: Ein Kulturbild* (Essen: Phaidon Verlag, 1997).

4   See Martin van Creveld, *On Future War* (London: Brassey's, 1991), pp. 50ff.

5   This transition did not take place all at once, of course, but there was already a considerable proportion of mercenaries in the medieval armies of the thirteenth and fourteenth centuries. See Rainer Wohlfeil, 'Das Heerwesen im Übergang vom Ritter-zum Söldnerheer', in Johannes Kunisch, ed., *Staatsverfassung und Heeresverfassung in der europäischen Geschichte der frühen Neuzeit*, in collaboration with Barbara Stollberg-Rillinger (Berlin: Duncker & Humblot, 1986), pp. 112ff.

6   See Robert Geoffrey Trease, *The Condottieri: Soldiers of Fortune* (London: Thames & Hudson, 1970). Of course, most condottieri did come from Italian ruling dynasties, such as the Montefeltre, Este, Gonzaga and others. Since they anyway had to wage war to defend their mini-state, they hired out to other states their troops and matériel (especially artillery) for periods when they did not need them, and usually offered themselves to command them. This had the further advantage of increasing their weight in the alliance policy of the Italian states beyond a level appropriate to the size of their own state.

7   See Willibald Block, *Die Condottieri: Studien über die so genannte 'unblütigen Schlachten'* (Berlin: E. Ebering, 1913).

8   Sacchetti, *Die wandernden Leuchtkäfer*, p. 81.

9   Niccolò Machiavelli, *The Prince* (London: Oxford University Press, 1935), pp. 54–5.

10   See Volker Schmidtchen, *Kriegswesen im späten Mittelalter: Technik, Taktik, Theorie* (Weinheim: VCH, Acta humaniora, 1990), pp. 231ff., and still also Hans Delbrück, *Geschichte der Kriegskunst im Rahmen der politischen Geschichte* (1920) (Berlin: de Gruyter, 2000), pp. 67ff. For a summary view, see also Volker Schmidtchen, 'Aspekte des Strukturwandels im europäischen Kriegswesen des späten Mittelalters und ihre Ursachen', in Ferdinand Seibt and Winfried Eberhard, eds, *1500: Integrationsprozesse im Widerstreit. Staaten, Regionen, Personenverbände, Christenheit* (Stuttgart: Klett-Cotta, 1987), pp. 445–67.

11   Delbrück, *Geschichte der Kriegskunst*, pp. 92ff., 106ff., 121ff.

12   According to Guicciardini's account, when Trivulzio was asked by the King of France which weapons and supplies would be needed to capture Milan, he answered: 'Tre cose, Sire, ci bisognano preparare danari, danari e poi danari!' ('Three things, sire, they need to provide for us: money, money and more money!'). This was Trivulzio's variation on the idea going back to Livy and Machiavelli that three things are necessary in war: a capable army, clever commanders and good fortune. See Michael Stolleis, *Pecunia Nervus Rerum: zur Staatsfinanzierung in der frühen Neuzeit* (Frankfurt am Main: Klostermann, 1983), pp. 64–5.

13 On the patterns of state revenue in the sixteenth and seventeenth centuries, see Michael Mann, *A History of Power from the Beginning to AD 1760*, vol. 1: *The Sources of Power* (Cambridge: Cambridge University Press, 1986), pp. 451–2; and Wolfgang Reinhard, *Geschichte der Staatsgewalt* (Munich: Beck, 1999), pp. 309ff.

14 For a summary picture see Baumann, *Landsknechte*, pp. 92ff., and for a more detailed analysis Peter Burschel, *Söldner im Nordwestdeutschland des 16. und 17. Jahrhunderts: Sozialgeschichtliche Studien*, Veröffentlichungen des Max-Planck-Instituts für Geschichte, vol. 113 (Göttingen: Vandenhoeck & Ruprecht, 1994). See also Brage Bei der Wieden, 'Niederdeutsche Söldner vor dem Dreißigjährigen Krieg: Geistige und mentale Grenzen des sozialen Raums', in Bernard Kroener and Ralf Pröve, eds, *Krieg und Frieden: Militär und Gesellschaft in der Frühen Neuzeit* (Paderborn: Schöningh, 1996), pp. 85–107 (with critical remarks on Burschel).

15 See Matthias Rogg, ' "Zerhauen und zerschnitten, nach adelichen Sitten": Herkunft, Entwicklung und Funktion soldatischer Tract des 16. Jahrhunderts im Spiegel zeitgenössischer Kunst', in Kroener and Pröve, *Krieg und Frieden*, pp. 109–35; and Rainer Trudl Wohlfeil, 'Das Landsknecht-Bild als geschichtiche Quelle: Überlegungen zur historischen Bildkunde', in Messerschmidt et al., eds, *Militärgeschichte: Probleme, Thesen, Wege* (Stuttgart: Deutsche Verlags-Anstalt, 1982), pp. 81–99.

16 For further discussion as well as bibliographical references, see Bernhard R. Kroener, ' "Das Schwungrad an der Staatsmachine"? Die Bedeutung der bewaffneten Macht in der europäischen Geschichte der Frühen Neuzeit', in Kroener and Pröve, *Krieg und Frieden*, pp. 1–23, here pp. 14ff; and id., 'Soldat oder Soldateska?', in Messerschmidt et al., *Militärgeschichte*, pp. 100–23, here pp. 111ff.

17 The contemporary term 'army-state' initially denoted no more than a special corporation or a part of the whole. As the statization process developed, however, the formula *'imperium in imperio'* (an empire within the empire) took on an increasingly negative significance. See Paul-Ludwig Weinacht, *Staat: Studien zur Bedeutungsgeschichte des Wortes von den Anfängen bis ins 19. Jahrhundert* (Berlin: Duncker & Humblot, 1968), pp. 107ff, 189–90.

18 A good example here is Luther's remark in his table conversations: 'Landsknechts among people are like a bloater among herrings. A spoiled herring gives a bloater, and a man of war gives something that is of no other use.' (*D. Martin Luthers Werke: Kritische Gesammtausgabe*, vol. 4, *Tischreden* (Weimar: Hermann Böhlaus, 1916), p. 600.)

19 See Gerhard Oestreich, 'Der römische Stoizismus und die oranische Heeresreform', in id., *Geist und Gestalt des frühmodernen Staates* (Berlin: Duncker & Humblot, 1969), pp. 11–34; Oestreich, 'Politischer Neustoizismus und Niederländische Bewegung in Europa und besonders in Brandenburg-Preußen', in *Geist and Gestalt*, pp. 101–56

(cf. Oestreich, *Neostoicism and the Origins of the Modern State* (Cambridge: Cambridge University Press, 1982)); and Wolfgang Reinhard, 'Humanismus und Militarismus: Antike-Rezeption und Kriegshandwerk in der oranischen Heeresreform', in Franz Josef Worstbrock, *Krieg und Frieden im Horizont des Renaissancehumanismus*, Report No. XIII of the Kommission für Humanismusforschung, (Weinheim: Acta Humaniora, VCH, 1986), pp. 185–204.

20   Michael Roberts, in his famous inaugural lecture at Queen's University, Belfast, used the term 'military revolution' to sum up these technological advances and tactical changes. See Michael Roberts, 'The military revolution, 1560–1660', in Clifford J. Rogers, ed., *The Military Revolution Debate: Readings on the Military Transformation of Early Modern Europe* (Boulder, Colo.: Westview Press, 1995), pp. 13–35. See also Geoffrey Parker, *The Military Revolution: Military Innovation and the Rise of the West, 1500–1800* (Cambridge: Cambridge University Press, 1996). And, on Spain's contribution to this revolution (which Roberts only touches upon), see Fernando González de Leon, ' "Doctors of the military discipline": Technical expertise and the paradigm of the Spanish soldier in the early modern period', *Sixteenth Century Journal*, 27, 1 (1996), pp. 61–85.

21   Weber himself never assumed such a strict determination of this trend as his followers have postulated. See Max Weber, *Wirtschaft und Gesellschaft*, ed. Johannes Winckelmann (Tübingen: Mohr, 1972), pp. 588ff.

22   For a summary of these trends, see Peter Burschel, 'Zur Sozialgeschichte innermilitärischer Disziplinierung', *Zeitschrift für Geschichtswissenschaft*, 42, 11 (1994), pp. 965–81.

23   For further detail, see Volker Schmidtchen, *Bombarden, Befestigungen, Büchsenmeister: Eine Studie zur Entwicklung der Militärtechnik* (Düsseldorf: Droste, 1977); and, more generally, John U. Nef, *Western Civilization since the Renaissance: Peace, War, Industry and the Arts* (New York: Harper & Row, 1963), pp. 23ff.

24   Max Weber, *Der Sozialismus*, ed. Herfried Münkler (Weinheim: Beltz, Athenäum, 1995), pp. 82–3.

25   See Simon Pepper and Nicholas Adams, *Firearms and Fortifications: Military Architecture and Siege Warfare in Sixteenth-Century Siena* (Chicago: University of Chicago Press, 1986).

26   See Werner Hahlweg, *Die Heeresreform der Oranier und die Antike* (1941) (Osnabrück: Biblio-Verlag, 1987).

27   See Reinhard, 'Humanismus und Militarismus', esp. pp. 194ff.

28   Max Weber established a strong connection between the state's standardized equipment of soldiers and the imposition of mass discipline: 'The separation of the warrior from the means of warfare, and the concentration of the means of warfare in the hands of the warlord have everywhere been basic to this mass discipline.' (Max Weber, *Economy and Society*, vol. 2 (Berkeley: University of California Press, 1968), p. 1155.)

29 The starting point for this debate is Michael Walzer's *Just and Unjust Wars: A Moral Argument with Historical Illustrations* (New York: Basic Books, 1977).

30 Michael Ignatieff, *The Warrior's Honour: Ethnic War and the Modern Conscience* (London: Chatto & Windus, 1998), pp. 109–64.

31 Of course, this in no way means that the practice of hiring out troops came to a complete end; only that private entrepreneurs no longer made a business out of it in the hope of raking in profits. Rather, states or sovereigns themselves hired out troops, in order to show something in the way of income to offset what they had already spent on them. The most famous example was the Landgrave of Hesse-Kassel, who hired out several regiments to the British at the time of the American War of Independence.

32 See Bernhard R. Kroener, 'Vom "extraordinari Kriegsvolck" zum "miles perpetuus"', *Militärgeschichtliche Mitteilungen*, 43, 1 (1988), pp. 141–87, esp. pp. 166ff.

33 On the growth in tax revenue, see (in addition to the works cited in note 13 above) Martin van Creveld, *The Rise and Decline of the State* (Cambridge: Cambridge University Press, 1999), pp. 147ff.; Michael Stolleis, *Pecunia Nervus Rerum*, pp. 103ff.; and Norbert Winnige, 'Von der Kontribution zur Akzise: Militärfinanzierung als Movens staatlicher Steuerpolitik', in Kroener and Pröve, *Krieg und Frieden*, pp. 59–83.

34 First published in German in 1948, the work to be consulted here is still Ludwig Dehio, *The Precarious Balance: The Politics of Power in Europe, 1494–1945* (London: Chatto & Windus, 1963), esp. pp. 50ff. Critical of the balance-of-power model but full of valuable information is Alfred Vagts, 'Die Chimäre des europäischen Gleichgewichts', in id., *Bilanzen und Balancen*, ed. Hans-Ulrich Wehler (Frankfurt am Main: Syndikat, 1979), pp. 131–60.

35 Certainly the most significant exception was the war in Spain from 1807 to 1813, in which the Napoleonic armies found themselves getting nowhere at all. Russia also resorted to partisan warfare against Napoleon (as it did later against Hitler), although it combined this with operations by regular armies. Both countries lay, of course, on the periphery of Europe.

36 See the synoptic overview in Paulus Engelhardt, 'Die Lehre vom "gerechten Krieg" in der vorreformatischen und katholischen Tradition', in Reiner Steinweg, ed., *Friedensanalysen*, vol. 12: *Der gerechte Krieg: Christentum, Islam, Marxismus* (Frankfurt am Main: Suhrkamp, 1980), pp. 72–123.

37 See Gerhard Beestermöller, *Thomas von Aquin und der gerechte Krieg: Friedensethik im theologischen Kontext der Summa theologiae* (Cologne: Bachem, 1990).

38 Gerhard Beestermöller underlines this ethic with an eye to current political constellations. See his ' "Rettet den Armen und befreit den Dürftigen aus der Hand des Sünders" (Ps. 82, 4). Thomas von Aquin

und die humanitäre Intervention', in Nils Goldschmidt, *Die Zukunft der Familie und deren Gefährdungen: Festschrift für Norbert Glatzel zum 65. Geburtstag* (Münster: Lit, 2002), pp. 401–19.

39   See Jörg Fisch, *Die europäische Expansion und das Völkerrecht: Die Auseinandersetzungen um den Status der überseeischen Gebiete vom 15. Jahrhundert bis zur Gegenwart* (Stuttgart: Steiner, 1984), esp. pp. 167ff. and 209–46.

40   See Otto Kimminich, 'Die Entstehung des neuzeitlichen Völkerrechts', in Iring Fetscher and Herfried Münkler, eds, *Pipers Handbuch der politischen Ideen*, vol. 3 (Munich: Piper, 1985), pp. 73–100, esp. pp. 84–5. In Wilhelm G. Grewe, *Epochen der Völkerrechtsgeschichte* (Baden-Baden: Nomos Verlag, 1984), pp. 247ff., the section on Gentili is entitled '*Bellum als duellum*' (cf. *The Epochs of International Law* (Berlin/New York: de Gruyter, 2000).

41   See Carl Schmitt, *Der Nomos der Erde im Völkerrecht des Jus Publicum Europaeum* (Cologne: Greven, 1950), pp. 111ff.

42   See Grewe, *Epochen der Völkerrechtsgeschichte*, pp. 245ff.; and van Creveld, *The Rise and Decline of the State*, pp. 161–2.

43   Carl von Clausewitz, *On War*, ed. Anatol Rapoport (Harmondsworth: Penguin Books, 1968), p. 348 (Book IV, chapter 12). Clausewitz brought this point to life from his own experience: 'Now it is known by experience, that the losses in physical forces in the course of a battle seldom present a great difference between victor and vanquished, often none at all, sometimes even one bearing an inverse relation to the result, and that the most decisive losses on the side of the vanquished only commence with the retreat, that is, those which the conqueror does not share with them. The weak remains of battalions already in disorder are cut down by cavalry, exhausted men strew the ground, disabled guns and broken caissons are abandoned, others in the bad state of the roads cannot be removed quickly enough, and are captured by the enemy's troops, during the night numbers lose their way, and fall defenceless into the enemy's hands, and thus the victory mostly gains bodily substance after it is already decided' (ibid., p. 309 (Book IV, chapter 4)).

44   The rise of the military within the social hierarchy would appear to be decisively correlated with the changes in warfare described above. Exaggerating a little, we might say that social recognition compensates for the loss of booty-taking opportunities. But this is reversed in the case of the new wars: since no social recognition is on offer, the concern for war booty is again unrestricted.

45   See Ute Frevert, *Die kasernierte Nation: Militärdienst und Zivilgesellschaft in Deutschland* (Munich: Beck, 2001), esp. pp. 39ff.

46   See Reinhard, 'Humanismus und Militarismus', pp. 191ff.

47   See Herfried Münkler, *Machiavelli: Die Begründung des politischen Denkens der Neuzeit aus der Krise der Republik Florenz* (Frankfurt am Main: Europäische Verlagsanstalt, 1982), pp. 381ff. This debate was held

again among the Scottish moral philosophers of the second half of the eighteenth century: see Matthias Bohlender, ' "Die Poetik der Schlacht und die Prosa des Krieges": Nationalverteidigung und Bürgermiliz im moralphilosophischen Diskurs der schottischen Aufklärung', *Die Wiedergeburt des Krieges aus dem Geiste der Revolution, Beiträge zur Politischen Wissenschaft* No. 110 (Berlin: 1999), pp. 17–41.

48 Volker Schmidtchen has illustrated this very precisely from the battle of Kortrijk (1302), the so-called Battle of the Spurs: see his 'Aspekte des Strukturwandels im europäischen Kriegswesen des späten Mittelalters', in Seibt and Eberhard, *1500*, pp. 451ff.

49 See Trutz von Trotha, 'Das Kalaschsyndrom: Gewalt zwischen Privatisierung, Männlichkeit, Jugend, Opferanspruch und massenmedialer Verherrlichung', *Frankfurter Rundschau*, 15 December 2001, p. 19; and Paul Richards, *Fighting for the Rain Forest: War, Youth and Resources in Sierra Leone* (Oxford: International African Institute, 1996).

50 See Herfried Münkler, *Der Partisan: Theorie, Strategie, Gestalt* (Opladen: Westdeutscher Verlag, 1990).

51 See the chapter 'Zwischen Entscheidungsschlacht und Partisanenkrieg: Clausewitz' Theorie des Krieges', in my *Über den Krieg: Stationen der Kriegsgeschichte im Spiegel ihrer theoretischen Reflexion* (Weilerswist: Velbrück, 2002), pp. 75–90.

52 Clausewitz, *On War* (Book VI, chapter 26).

53 Ibid.

54 See Wolfgang Schivelbusch, *Die Kultur der Niederlage* (Berlin: A. Fest Verlag, 2001), pp. 133ff.

55 The only really major changes were the disappearance of Poland from the European map at the end of the eighteenth century and the creation of the German Reich in 1871, resulting in shifts in the balance of power and adjustments to military scenarios.

56 Christopher Daase has tried to show that this applies not only to arms policy but also to the conduct of war: see his *Kleine Kriege – Große Wirkung: Wie unkonventionelle Kriegsführung die internationale Politik verändert* (Baden-Baden: Nomos Verlag, 1999), pp. 91ff.

57 For a concise summary, see Werner Gembruch, 'Die preußischen Reformer', in Fetscher and Münkler, eds, *Pipers Handbuch*, vol. 4, pp. 79–91.

58 See two recent works: Roger Chickering, *Imperial Germany and the Great War, 1914–1918* (Cambridge: Cambridge University Press, 1998), pp. 32ff., 96ff.; and John Keegan, *The First World War* (London: Hutchinson, 1998), pp. 223ff.

59 See Mary Kaldor, *The Imaginary War: Understanding the East–West Conflict* (Oxford: Blackwell, 1990), pp. 191ff.; and Michael Salewski, ed., *Das Zeitalter der Bombe: Die Geschichte der atomaren Bedrohung von Hiroshima bis heute* (Munich: Beck, 1995).

60 The history of war continued in the background, of course, although it could no longer be 'waged' but only 'conceptualized'. Instead of the

physical annihilation of enemy weapons systems in battle, the aim was to devalue them by means of an arms race. Thus it was advances in microelectronics which, from the early 1980s, caused the Soviet Union to fall ever further behind so that, by the middle of the decade, it had become clear to the Soviet leadership that it was no longer economically or technologically capable of matching the military capability of the United States.

61 See Anita and Walter Dietze, eds, *Ewiger Friede? Dokumente einer deutschen Diskussion um 1880* (Munich: Beck, 1989); Claudius R. Fischbach, *Krieg und Frieden in der Französischen Aufklärung* (Münster/New York: Wazamann, 1990).

62 Immanuel Kant, 'Perpetual peace: A philosophical sketch', in id., *Political Writings*, 2nd enlarged edn (Cambridge: Cambridge University Press, 1991), p. 114.

63 Ibid. It is remarkable that, in most of the recent interpretations of Kant's text that are rooted in legal theory or moral philosophy, scarcely any attention is paid to its strong social and economic foundations.

64 Relevant passages from Comte and Spencer may be found in Günther Wachtler, ed., *Militär, Krieg, Gesellschaft: Texte zur Militärsoziologie* (Darmstadt: Wissenschaftliche Buchgesellschaft, 1983), pp. 27ff., 38ff.

65 Joseph A. Schumpeter, *Capitalism, Socialism and Democracy*, 5th edn (London: George Allen & Unwin, 1976), p. 128.

66 See Michael Howard, *The Invention of Peace: Reflections on War and International Order* (London: Profile, 2000), pp. 98–102.

67 Kant, 'Perpetual peace', p. 100.

68 On the postulate of democratic peace, see Michael E. Brown, Sean M. Lynn-Jones and Steven E. Miller, eds, *Debating the Democratic Peace* (Cambridge, Mass.: MIT Press, 1996); and Thomas Risse-Kappen, 'Wie weiter mit dem "demokratischen Frieden"?', *Zeitschrift für internationale Beziehungen*, 1 (1994), pp. 367–79.

69 Representative of many in this respect are Klaus Jürgen Gantzel, 'Kriegsursachen – Tendenzen und Pespektiven', *Ethik und Sozialwissenschaften*, 8, 3 (1997), pp. 257–66; and Dieter Senghaas, ed., *Den Frieden denken: Si vis pacem, para pacem* (Frankfurt am Main: Suhrkamp, 1995), esp. pp. 196–223.

Chapter 4 The Economics of Force in the New Wars

1 Peter Lock, 'Light weapons and conflict in Africa', *Peace and Security: The ILP Research Quarterly*, 331 (December 1999), pp. 31–6, esp. p. 35. The cheapness of old-style kalashnikovs, in particular, also has something to do with their indestructibility, since this means that they often go for a song in a market where new models are constantly appearing.

2 'Today, handheld automatic weapons are short and light, the newer models increasingly resembling children's toys. The old Mauser was too long, too big, and too heavy for a child. A child's small arm could not reach freely for the trigger, and he had difficulty taking aim. Modern design has solved these problems, eliminated the inconveniences. The dimensions of weapons are now perfectly suited to a boy's physique, so much so that in the hands of tall, massive men, the new guns appear somewhat comical and childish.' (Ryszard Kapuściński, *The Shadow of the Sun: My African Life* (London: Allen Lane, 2001), p. 149.)

3 These differences between new and classical wars are the reason why the latter are also known as 'postmodern wars'. See, for example, Mark Duffield, 'Post-modern conflict: Warlords, post-adjustment states and private protection', *Civil Wars*, 1, 1 (1998), pp. 65–102.

4 See chapter 1, pp. 8–10.

5 Peter Lock, 'Privatisierung der Sicherheit im Spannungsfeld zunehmend gewaltoffener Räume und staatlichen Gewaltmonopols: Thesen zur sozialen Apartheid', in Österreichisches Studienzentrum für Frieden und Konfliktlösung, ed., *Wie sicher ist Europa?* (Münster: Agenda, 2001), pp. 65–78, here p. 75.

6 Ahmed Rashid, *Taliban: The Story of the Afghan Warlords* (London: Pan Books, 2001), p. 109.

7 'In front of the Alliance's recruitment office', reported Hans Christoph Buch from a disintegrating Zaire, 'a lively throng of children and young people are voluntarily registering to fight, because it is their only way of getting food and clothing. They are bent on joining the rebel army that has already, at Kisangani airport, inflicted a crushing defeat on the Zaire army and the mercenaries in the pay of Mobutu.' (*Blut im Schuh: Schlächter und Voyeure an den Fronten des Weltbürgerkriegs* (Frankfurt am Main: Eichborn, 2001), p. 258.)

8 Lock, 'Privatisierung der Sicherheit', p. 74.

9 Peter Scholl-Latour, *Afrikanische Totenklage: Der Ausverkauf des Schwarzen Kontinents* (Munich: Bertelsmann, 2001), p. 425. Hans Christoph Buch reports similar evidence from Liberia: 'Things become dangerous at midday, once the boy soldiers of the NPFL have fired themselves up with Dutch courage; they gesticulate with their weapons, and only with difficulty can they be kept from executing a prisoner in front of the camera.' (Buch, *Blut im Schuh*, p. 234.)

10 Rashid, *Taliban*, p. 73.

11 David Rieff, *Slaughterhouse: Bosnia and the Failure of the West* (New York: Simon & Schuster, 1995), p. 130. Zlatko Dizdarević has described in meticulous detail the moral decay which, in the first year of the siege of Sarajevo, affected the layers and groups who are traditionally at the heart of a functioning civil society. See his *Sarajevo: A War Journal* (New York: Henry Holt, 1994).

12 For the age of the condottieri in Italy, it has been noted that banditry declined in time of war and grew again in peacetime. See Reinhard,

Geschichte der Staatsgewalt (Munich: Beck, 1999), p. 346. This is also true of the new wars, except that in this case the line of demarcation is not so marked.

13   Warlords in both Liberia and Sierra Leone stirred up armed young-sters with cheap drugs. Scholl-Latour (*Afrikanische Totenklage*, p. 366) quotes a Human Rights Watch report on what it considers a typical case: after joining a combat unit, a boy killed first his former teacher (who had given him a bad mark) and then his former employer (who had paid him badly). Subsequently, he raped the mothers of his former friends.

14   Machiavelli is well known for his advice that, in keeping with the model of Cesare Borgia, a ruler who has come to power through luck and violence must put to death his colonels and captains, since the situa-tion would in many respects be comparable to the one he had himself previously faced and it would be necessary to block the path of any would-be imitators.

15   A good example here is ethnologist Hans Peter Duerr's broadly con-ceived alternative to Norbert Elias's theory of a slow but steadily advancing process of human self-civilization. For Duerr, human be-haviour remains always the same in substance, though not necessarily in form – with wartime violence against women a very important case in point. See his *Der Mythos vom Zivilisationsprozess*, vol. 3: *Obszönität und Gewalt* (Frankfurt am Main: Suhrkamp, 1993), pp. 242ff., 319ff., 363ff., 391ff., 428ff.

16   See Stefan Winkle, *Geißeln der Menschheit: Kulturgeschichte der Seuchen* (Düsseldorf: Artemis & Winkler, 1977), pp. 570ff.

17   Article 27, *Geneva Convention relative to the Protection of Civilian Persons in Time of War*, published by the Office of the High Commissioner for Human Rights, online at http://www.unhchr.ch/html/menu3/b/92.htm.

18   Ibid., Article 29. This convention, which came into force on 21 October 1950, had been ratified by Yugoslavia on 21 April 1950. On the conven-tion and further relevant provisions of international law, see Helga Wullweber, 'Vergewaltigung als Waffe und das Kriegsvölkerrecht', *Kritische Justiz*, 26 (1993), pp. 179–93.

19   Quoted from Maria Welser, *Am Ende wünschst du dir nur noch den Tod: Die Massenvergewaltigungen im Krieg auf dem Balkan* (Munich: Knaur, 1993), p. 149.

20   See Wolfgang Sofsky, *Violence, Terrorism, Genocide, War* (London: Granta Books, 2003), pp. 167ff.

21   See Noam Chomsky, *A New Generation Draws the Line: Kosovo, East Timor and the Standards of the West* (London: Verso, 2000), pp. 70ff.

22   One of the few twentieth-century accounts in which these events in the Balkans and Asia Minor are seen as central to the future course of European history is Dan Diner, *Das Jahrhundert verstehen: Eine universalhistorische Deutung* (Munich: Luchterhand, 1999), esp. pp. 195ff.

23 See Hannes Heer and Klaus Naumann, eds, *Vernichtungskrieg: Ver-brechen der Wehrmacht 1941–1944* (Hamburg: Hamburger Edition, 1995).

24 See Silva Meznaric, 'Gender as an ethno-marker: Rape, war, and identity politics in the former Yugoslavia', in Valentine M. Moghadam, ed., *Identity Politics and Women: Cultural Reassertions and Feminisms in International Perspective* (Boulder, Colo.: Westview Press, 1994), pp. 76–97; Julie Moscow, ' "Our women"/"their women": Symbolic boundaries, territorial markers, and violence in the Balkans', *Peace and Change*, 20, 4 (1995), pp. 515–29; and Slavenka Drakulić, 'The rape of women in Bosnia', in *Women and Violence*, compiled by Miranda Davies (London: Zed Books, 1994), pp. 176–81.

25 'Before the beginning of the fighting, there had been approximately a thousand mosques in Bosanska Krajina. By the winter of 1994, there were certainly no more than a hundred and probably far fewer.' (David Rieff, *Slaughterhouse*, p. 97.)

26 See Ruth Seifert, 'Der weibliche Körper als Symbol und Zeichen: Geschlechtsspezifische Gewalt und die kulturelle Konstruktion des Krieges', in Andreas Gestrich, ed., *Gewalt im Krieg: Ausübung, Erfahrung und Verweigerung von Gewalt in Kriegen des 20. Jahrhunderts* (Munich: Lit, 1996), pp. 12–33, here pp. 28–9.

27 See chapter 1, p. 14.

28 See chapter 2, pp. 42ff.

29 See chapter 2, pp. 32–4.

30 Susan Brownmiller, *Against Our Will: Men, Women and Rape* (London: Secker & Warburg, 1975), p. 38; and, more recently, Claudia Opitz, 'Von Frauen im Krieg zum Krieg gegen Frauen: Krieg, Gewalt und Geschlechtsbeziehungen aus historischer Sicht', *L'Homme*, 3, 1 (1992), pp. 31–44, here pp. 40ff.

31 See also Seifert, 'Der weibliche Körper', p. 26.

32 On the distinction between societies with a high and societies with a low incidence of rape, see ibid., p. 15, where a low figure is attributed to a notoriously weak position of women and a lack of challenges to the strong position of men.

33 On the rapes in Bangladesh, see Kevin Gerard Neill, 'Duty, honor, rape: Sexual assault against women during war', *Journal of International Women's Studies*, 2, 1 (2001); and on the rapes in northern Afghanistan, see Rashid, *Taliban*, p. 107.

34 Buch, *Blut im Schuh*, pp. 170, 303.

35 See Clotilde Twagiramariya and Meredeth Turshen, ' "Favors" to give and "consenting" victims: The sexual politics of survival in Rwanda', in *What Women Do in Wartime: Gender and Conflict in Africa* (London/New York: 1998), pp. 101–17.

36 See the entries in the volumes for 1999 and 2000 produced by the Hamburg-based working group on the causes of war, Arbeitsgemein-schaft Kriegsursachenforschung.

37 This dimension of the use of force is at the centre of Sofsky's analysis in *Violence, Terrorism, Genocide, War*, esp. pp. 93ff., 134ff., 151ff.

38 Ibid., pp. 165–6.
39 See, for example, Wullweber, 'Vergewaltigung als Waffe', pp. 182–3.
40 Rieff, *Slaughterhouse*, p. 107.
41 Sexual violence, or at least the rape of women and sometimes the cas-
    tration of men, is especially common where the belligerents may be
    classed as belonging to different ethnic or religious communities. In
    the American Civil War, as in the Vietnam War on the Vietcong side,
    rape was not one of the means used to humiliate or intimidate the
    enemy.
42 Lock, 'Privatisierung der Sicherheit', p. 74.
43 For a critical balance sheet of the link between humanitarian aid and
    civil war economies, see John Prendergast, *Frontline Diplomacy: Hu-
    manitarian Aid and Conflict in Africa* (Boulder, Colo.: Lynne Rienner,
    1996); and François Jean, 'Aide humanitaire et économie de guerre',
    in François Jean and Jean-Christophe Rufin, eds, *Économie des guerres
    civiles* (Paris: Hachette, 1996), pp. 543–89.
44 Rieff, *Slaughterhouse*, p. 88.
45 For a more detailed discussion of these points, see Mary B.
    Anderson, *Do No Harm: How Aid Can Support Peace – or War* (Boulder,
    Colo.: Lynne Rienner, 1999); and David Keen and Ken Wilson, 'En-
    gaging with violence: A reassessment of relief in wartime', in Joanna
    Macrae and Anthony Zwi, eds, *War and Hunger: Rethinking International
    Responses to Complex Emergencies* (London: Zed Books, 1994), pp. 209–
    21.
46 Michael Birnbaum, *Krisenherd Somalia: Das Land des Terrors und der An-
    archie* (Munich: Heyne, 2002), pp. 93–4.
47 See Christopher Daase, *Kleine Kriege – Große Wirkung: Wie unkonven-
    tionelle Kriegführung die internationale Politik verändert* (Baden-Baden:
    Nomos Verlag, 1999), pp. 196ff.
48 Ibid., pp. 173ff.
49 This is how one author sums up the Balkan wars of the 1990s: 'The
    whole war was evidently fought by means of television. The Ameri-
    can President ordered NATO attacks after he had seen a CNN report
    about the shooting of three children on a sledge; he no longer needed
    reports from his secret services about the real situation on the ground.
    It was now all about appearances, about theatrical presentation. It no
    longer seems possible to find the truth.' (Paolo Rumiz, *Masken für ein
    Massaker: Der manipulierte Krieg. Spurensuche auf dem Balkan* (Munich:
    Kunstmann, 2000), pp. 47–8. Original: *Maschere per un massacro* (Rome:
    Riuniti, 1996).)
50 See Mark Duffield, 'The political economy of internal war: Asset trans-
    fer, complex emergencies and international aid', in Macrae and Zwi,
    War and Hunger, pp. 50–69; and Jean-Christophe Rufin, 'Les économies
    de guerre dans les conflits internes', in Jean and Rufin, *Économie*.
51 See Michael Riekenberg, 'Warlords', *Comparativ*, 5–6 (1999), pp. 187–205.

52   Cf. Mats Berdal and David Keen, 'Violence and economic agendas in civil wars: Some policy implications', *Millennium: Journal of International Studies*, 26, 3 (1997), pp. 795–818.

53   On this and the following points, see Barnett R. Rubin, *The Political Economy of War and Peace in Afghanistan* (New York: Council on Foreign Relations, 1999).

54   Rashid, *Taliban*, pp. 117, 121.

55   Ibid., pp. 21–2.

56   This definition of informal economies is borrowed from Lock, 'Privatisierung der Sicherheit', p. 69.

57   See Nazih F. Richani, 'The political economy of violence: The war-system in Colombia', *Journal of Interamerican Studies and World Affairs*, 39, 2 (1997), pp. 37–82.

58   See William Reno, *Warlord Politics and African States* (Boulder, Colo.: Lynne Rienner, 1998).

59   See Riekenberg, 'Warlords', pp. 191ff.

60   See Alain Labrousse, 'Territoire et réseaux: l'exemple de la drogue en Pérou–Colombie. Violence politique et logique criminelle', in Jean and Rufin, *Économie*; John Simpson, *In the Forests of the Night: Encounters in Peru with Terrorism, Drug-running and Military Oppression* (London: Hutchinson, 1993); and Mauricio Rubio, *Conflict, Crime and Violence in Colombia* (Washington, DC: World Bank, 1999).

61   The term 'interested third party' was first used by Rolf Schroers to describe such a supportive outside power (*Der Partisan: Ein Beitrag zur politischen Anthropologie* (Cologne: Kiepenheuer & Witsch, 1961), pp. 247ff.), having originally been introduced in a wider context by Carl Schmitt (*Theorie des Partisanen: Zwischenbemerkung zum Begriff des Politischen* (Berlin: Duncker & Humblot, 1963), p. 78).

62   The Cuban expeditionary corps was, of course, only a response to the massive intervention by South African troops in the Angolan civil war.

63   See Berndt Georg Thamm, 'Rauschgift, Terror und Konflikte: Drogenkapital und aktuelles Kriegsgeschehen', *Suchtreport*, 3 (2000), pp. 4–11.

64   Cf. Pierre Kopp, 'Embargo et criminalisation économique', in Jean and Rufin, *Économie*.

65   The Kosovo–Albanian UCK (Kosovo Liberation Army) funded its war mainly from the drugs trade and prostitution in Western Europe: cf. Jürgen Roth, *Netzwerke des Terrors* (Hamburg: Europa Verlag, 2001), pp. 182ff.

66   See the section on 'sexual enslavement' in Pino Arlacchi, *Ware Mensch: Der Skandal des modernen Sklavenhandels* (Munich: Piper, 1999), pp. 83ff. War zones are a good reservoir for the increasing demand for sex slaves, and here too an intensive interaction is apparent between peace-economy markets and supplies made available by war economies.

Chapter 5   International Terrorism

1   Carl von Clausewitz, *On War*, ed. Anatol Rapoport (Harmondsworth: Penguin Books, 1968), p. 101 (Book I, chapter 1).

2   This aspect is brought out most clearly in David Fromkin, 'Die Strategie des Terrorismus', in Manfred Funke, ed., *Terrorismus: Untersuchungen zur Strategie und Struktur revolutionärer Gewaltpolitik* (Bonn: Bundeszentrale für Politische Bildung, 1977), pp. 83–99, esp. pp. 93ff. For a summary of the issues, see also Herfried Münkler, 'Guerrillakrieg und Terrorismus', *Neue Politische Literatur*, 25, 3 (1980), pp. 299–326.

3   See Peter Waldmann, *Terrorismus: Provokation der Macht* (Munich: Gerling, 1998), pp. 48–9; and Bruce Hoffman, *Inside Terrorism* (London: Gollancz, 1998), pp. 131ff.

4   Clausewitz, *On War*, p. 309 (Book IV, chapter 4).

5   It has become commonplace in journalistic commentary to associate terrorism with cowardice, but what is really meant is recourse to underhand wiles.

6   See chapter 4, pp. 96ff.

7   See Gilles Kepel, *Jihad: The Trail of Political Islam* (London: I. B. Tauris, 2003), pp. 299ff.

8   See Walter Laqueur, *Terrorism* (London: Abacus, 1978), pp. 13–32. Cf. Caleb Carr, *The Lessons of Terror: A History of Warfare against Civilians. Why It Has Always Failed, and Why It Will Fail Again* (London: Little, Brown, 2002), who uses a very imprecise concept of terror and argues that terrorist tactics and strategy are doomed to fail.

9   Laqueur, *Terrorism*, pp. 33–99.

10   See André Beaufre, *La Guerre révolutionnaire: Les formes nouvelles de la guerre* (Paris: Fayard, 1972), esp. pp. 273ff.

11   Hoffman, *Inside Terrorism*, pp. 45–66.

12   A more precise distinction should be drawn here, as in most other cases, between the official legitimation and the original motivation of terrorist groups. Thus, many terrorist groups that later claimed an Islamic legitimacy attached little or no significance to religious aspects in the early stages of their development; only under the impact of a number of failures did this dimension greatly contribute to their further radicalization. Cf. Mark Juergensmeyer, *Terror in the Mind of God: The Global Rise of Religious Violence* (Berkeley: University of California Press, 2000).

13   Cf. Hoffman, *Inside Terrorism*, pp. 87–130; Waldmann, *Terrorismus*, pp. 98–119; and Walter Laqueur, *The New Terrorism: Fanaticism and the Arms of Mass Destruction* (New York: Oxford University Press, 1999), pp. 184–209.

14   See Oliver Schröm, *Im Schatten des Schakals: Carlos und die Wegbereiter des internationalen Terrorismus* (Berlin: Links, 2002) – a work based on journalistic sources which contains a wealth of background information, and which also gives a detailed account of the participation of

German terrorists from the so-called Revolutionary Cells in Palestinian operations. According to Schröm, the 'allies' almost always served to escalate the violence.

15 It is possible that this observation rests upon a Europe-centred fore-shortening that has gradually taken in the (often European-influenced) history of war elsewhere. Without exception, 'small war' strategists have played a much more important role outside Europe than they did in Europe from the seventeenth to the twentieth century. The growing political and military significance of these regions, or perhaps simply the media-produced extension of our field of observation, is therefore the reason why the history of war in the past half-century appears to us as a process which has freed tactical elements that were originally tied to and subordinated to the level of strategy.

16 See chapter 2, pp. 34–41.

17 Mao Zedong's innovation vis-à-vis traditional strategies of partisan warfare – at least as seen from a European perspective – was that he no longer conceived of small and large war as simultaneous with each other. In his theory, partisan warfare was a phase of preparation and training for the war which would eventually be fought with regular forces that grew out of the partisan units.

18 See Waldmann, *Terrorismus*, pp. 56ff.; and Hoffman, *Inside Terrorism*, pp. 131ff.

19 Of course, this trend already began with the industrialization of the war machine, which meant that workers in the belligerent states became 'semi-combatants'. This was the basis for the wartime British–American strategy of bombing not only production sites but especially workers' districts in Germany. On the implications for morality and international law, see Michael Walzer, *Just and Unjust Wars: A Moral Argument with Historical Illustrations* (London: Allen Lane, 1978), pp. 255–62.

20 Carl Schmitt, *Theorie des Partisanen: Zwischenbemerkung zum Begriff des Politischen* (Berlin: Duncker & Humblot, 1963), p. 20.

21 Recently, it has been suggested in a number of publications that China has the potential to become a symmetrical challenger of the United States. The Chinese, however, do not see things in this way, but start from the assumption that a conflict with the United States would take the form of asymmetrical warfare. For example, two officers in the People's Liberation Army recently published a study in which they 'propose tactics for developing countries, in particular China, to compensate for their military inferiority vis-à-vis the United States during a high-tech war'. (Qiao Liang and Wang Xiangsui, *Unrestricted Warfare* (Beijing: PLA Literature and Arts Publishing House, February 1999) contains excerpts in English.)

22 See Gabriel Kolko, *Anatomy of a War: Vietnam, the United States, and the Modern Historical Experience* (New York: Pantheon Books, 1985).

23 The definition of terrorism given above applies not to the hostilities in which probably more than a thousand (sometimes armed but mostly

unarmed) Somalis were killed but to the stripping and mutilation of dead soldiers in the expectation that the cameras will film them and broadcast the pictures throughout the world. The fighting in connection with the failed arrest of Aidid followed the model of partisan warfare; the 'celebration of victory with corpses', however, was a stage-show for the international public designed only to sow terror. In the previous weeks Aidid's tactic had evidently been to provoke a massacre of Somali civilians by UN forces, with the aim of exploiting this for his own propaganda. See Michael Birnbaum, *Krisenherd Somalia: Das Land des Terrors und der Anarchie* (Munich: Heyne, 2002), 108ff.

24 See Peter Bergen, *Heiliger Krieg, Inc.: Osama Bin Ladens Terrornetz* (Berlin: Berliner Taschenbuch-Verlag, 2001), pp. 105–6.

25 See chapter 3, pp. 51ff.

26 Cf. Shlomo Shpiro, 'Medien und Terrorismus', *Internationale Politik*, 56, 12 (2001), pp. 19–24; and 'Conflict media strategies and the politics of counter-terrorism', *Politics*, 22, 2 (2002), pp. 76–85.

27 See Franklin L. Ford, *Political Murder: From Tyrannicide to Terrorism* (Cambridge, Mass.: Harvard University Press, 1985), pp. 216–38.

28 See Laqueur, *The New Terrorism*, pp. 49–78.

29 Cf. Waldmann, *Terrorismus*, pp. 23–4; Laqueur, *The New Terrorism*, pp. 238ff.

Chapter 6   Military Interventions and the West's Dilemma

1 See, for example, Jack Levy, 'Domestic politics and war', *Journal of Interdisciplinary History*, 18, 4 (1988), pp. 653–73; Michael E. Brown, Sean M. Lynn-Jones and Steven E. Miller, eds, *Debating the Democratic Peace* (Cambridge., Mass.: MIT Press, 1996); Thomas Risse-Kappen, 'Wie weiter mit dem "demokratischen Frieden"?', *Zeitschrift für internationale Beziehungen*, 1, 1994, pp. 367–79.

2 See, for example, Ernst-Otto Czempiel, *Kluge Macht: Außenpolitik für das 21. Jahrhundert* (Munich: Beck, 1999), esp. pp. 70ff.

3 An example of this systematic neglect of the cost problem is Ernst-Otto Czempiel's synthesis of the democratic peace theory, in *Neue Sicherheit in Europa: Eine Kritik an Neorealismus und Realpolitik* (Frankfurt am Main: Campus, 2002), p. 33: 'The reason' [why 'democracies have never fought against one another'] 'lies first in the norms of conduct and then in the structure of the decision-making process. Democratic norms involving non-violence, compromise and the balancing of interests are pursued by the democracies in their external behaviour. The separation of powers creates so many barriers for a political system tending towards the use of force that society has sufficient possibilities of control and obstruction.'

4 See chapter 4, pp. 74–81.

5   An example of this is the focus on oil and gas reserves in the Middle East or Central Asia as a way of explaining the military involvement of Western powers (especially the United States) in those regions.

6   See Dieter Storz, *Kriegsbild und Rüstung vor 1914: Europäische Land-streitkräfte vor dem Ersten Weltkrieg*, 'Militärgeschichte und Wehrwis-senschaften' series, vol. 1 (Herford: Mittler, 1992).

7   Johann von Bloch, *Die wahrscheinlichen politischen und militärischen Folgen eines Krieges zwischen Grossmächten* (Berlin: 1901). Engels's warning of the catastrophic consequences of a great war in Europe may be found especially in his 1895 preface to Marx's *Class Struggles in France* (in Karl Marx and Friedrich Engels, *Selected Works* (London: Lawrence & Wishart, 1970), pp. 641–58, esp. p. 648). See also the chapter 'Dialektik des Militarismus oder Hegung des Krieges', in my *Über den Krieg: Stationen der Kriegsgeschichte im Spiegel ihrer theoretischen Reflexion* (Weilerweist: Velbrück, 2002) pp. 116–48.

8   These figures are taken from Gabriel Kolko, *Century of War: Politics, Conflicts, and Society since 1914* (New York: New Press, 1994), pp. 87–93. On the evolution of German society during the war years, see Volker Ullrich, 'Kriegsalltag: Zur inneren Revolutionierung der Wilhelmini-schen Gesellschaft', in Wolfgang Michalka, ed., *Der Erste Weltkrieg: Wirkung, Wahrnehmung, Analyse* (Munich: Piper, 1994), pp. 603–21; and Roger Chickering, *Imperial Germany and the Great War, 1914–1918* (Cambridge: Cambridge University Press, 1998), pp. 95ff.

9   Kolko, *Century of War*, p. 103.

10 On the slow collapse of armies and the open mutiny among sections of troops, see John Keegan, *The First World War* (London: Hutchin-son, 1998), pp. 333–98; Marc Ferro, *The Great War 1914–1918* (London: Routledge & Kegan Paul, 1987), pp. 180–8; and Kolko, *Century of War*, pp. 135ff.

11 One of the most revealing works on the collapse of France is Marc Bloch's *Strange Defeat* (London: Oxford University Press, 1949). Bloch's analysis ends with a wish reminiscent of Clausewitz's memorandum of 1812: 'My only hope . . . is that when the moment comes we shall have enough blood left to shed, even if it be the blood of those who are dear to us (I say nothing of my own, to which I attach no importance). For there can be no salvation where there is not some sacrifice, and no national liberty in the fullest sense unless we have ourselves worked to bring it about' (p. 175).

12 Leaving aside the totalitarian regimes of Nazi Germany and the Soviet Union, we may say that the willingness to fight on the part of the former 1914–18 belligerents was rather limited – with all due regard for Britain and the United States. It should be remembered, of course, that the latter two countries felt able to open a second front in the West (as Stalin had persistently demanded of them) only when the Wehrmacht's fighting capacity was already on the wane and the Allied air force had complete command of the skies over the frontline areas.

13 Popular accounts of the First World War mostly overlook the fact that the French too had a concept of the offensive, and that in early August 1914 the French army launched a broad offensive in Lorraine and Alsace. See Keegan, *The First World War*, pp. 97ff., and Ferro, *The Great War*.

14 For a critical look at the Blitzkrieg strategy, see Karl-Heinz Frieser, 'Die deutschen Blitzkriege: Operativer Triumph – strategische Tragödie', in Rolf-Dieter Müller and Hans-Erich Volkmann, eds, *Die Wehrmacht: Mythos und Realität* (Munich: Oldenbourg, 1999), pp. 182–96. Frieser denies Blitzkrieg the quality of a strategy and reduces it to a 'military-tactical phenomenon'. He here refers back to his earlier analysis of the so-called Western campaign of 1940 (*Blitzkrieg-Legende: Der Westfeldzug 1940* (Munich: Oldenbourg, 1995)), in which he depicted the fortuitous nature of military events in May–June 1940. Frieser's argument is based, however, on a strained concept of strategy and the evaluation of a single camapign. A comparative study of the campaigns between 1939 and 1942 would probably lead to a different conclusion. See, for example, Basil Henry Liddell Hart, *History of the Second World War* (London: Cassell, 1970), pp. 21, 27ff. Liddell Hart refers to similar strategic considerations in Britain which did not, however, take effect.

15 See Dilip Hiro, *The Longest War: The Iran–Iraq Military Conflict* (New York: Routledge, 1991). In this war, the Iranian side deployed suicide units for the first time on a grand scale – or, at any rate, it sent children into mined areas so that they could clear a way for the units following them. See Christoph Reuter, *Mein Leben ist eine Waffe: Selbstmordattentäter – Psychogramm eines Phänomens* (Munich: Bertelsmann, 2002), pp. 58ff.

16 The defensive strategy was not limited to France. Czechoslovakia built a similar fortified belt on its Western frontier, and Belgium and the Netherlands on their Eastern frontier, and even Nazi Germany put in place a so-called West Wall and later an Atlantic Wall. The great hopes that the Germans had of the latter are analysed in Michael Salewski, 'Die Abwehr der Invasion als Schlüssel zum "Endsieg"?', in Müller and Volkmann, *Die Wehrmacht*, pp. 210–23.

17 From the abundant literature, we shall simply mention here Max Hastings, *Bomber Command* (London: Joseph, 1979); and Richard Overy, *Why the Allies Won* (London: Jonathan Cape, 1995), pp. 101ff.

18 The bombing of workers' districts was intended to increase the slack time in factories, and also – since workers were unable to sleep at night – to increase the percentage of rejects in the arms industry. A 1944 report by the British air command expressed in figures the strategic purpose of the bombing war: 'To express these [German] losses in a different way, we might say that 2,400,000,000 working hours were lost for the price of 116,500 tons of bombs – which means that each ton was equivalent to 20,500 lost working hours, or a little more than a quarter of the time necessary to make a Lancaster aircraft. . . . This means that a Lancaster

had to reach a German city only once to recover its production costs; any further mission brought in pure profit.' (Quoted (and retranslated) from Peter Englund, *Menschheit am Nullpunkt: Aus dem Abgrund des 20. Jahrhunderts* (Stuttgart: Klett-Cotta, 2001), pp. 203–4.)

19   The Luftwaffe lacked the long-range heavy bombers to launch a strategic air war of its own; the so-called Battle of Britain had another strategic objective. The rocket attacks on London in the concluding phase of the war were a different matter, of course.

20   See Daniel Eisermann, 'Bomben für den Frieden? Die militärische Diplomatie der Nato und die Durchsetzung einer Friedensordnung im ehemaligen Jugoslawien', in Rüdiger Voigt, ed., *Krieg – Instrument der Politik? Bewaffnete Konflikte im Übergang vom 20. zum 21. Jahrhundert* (Baden-Baden: Nomos Verlag, 2002), pp. 131–59, here esp. pp. 151–2.

21   Cf. Michael Ignatieff, *Virtual War: Kosovo and Beyond* (London: Chatto & Windus, 2000), pp. 161ff.

22   Figures for these wars may be found in Klaus Jürgen Gantzel, 'Über die Kriege nach dem Zweiten Weltkrieg', in Bernd Wegner, ed., *Wie Kriege entstehen: Zum historischen Hintergrund von Staatenkonflikten* (Paderborn: Schöningh, 2000), pp. 299–318, esp. pp. 302ff.

23   On the battle of Omdurman, see Victor G. Kiernan, *European Empires from Conquest to Collapse, 1815–1960* (London: Fontana, 1982), pp. 79–80.

24   See John Ellis, *The Social History of the Machine Gun* (London: Croom Helm, 1975).

25   Once again, the consequences are most impressively described by John Keegan. See his *The Face of Battle* (London: Cape, 1976), pp. 242–336, esp. pp. 285ff.

26   See Martin van Creveld, *On Future War* (London: Brassey's, 1991), pp. 24ff.

27   See chapter 5, pp. 106ff.

28   See Ullrich Bartosch, *Weltinnenpolitik: Zur Theorie des Friedens von Carl Friedrich von Weizsäcker* (Berlin: Duncker & Humblot, 1995), esp. pp. 238ff.

29   Jürgen Habermas, 'Bestialität und Humanität', in Reinhard Merkel, ed., *Der Kosovo-Krieg und das Völkerrecht* (Frankfurt am Main: Suhrkamp, 2000), pp. 51–65, here p. 61.

30   Noam Chomsky, *Rogue States* (London: Pluto Press, 2000), esp. pp. 124–55.

31   Ulrich Beck, 'Über den postnationalen Krieg', *Blätter für deutsche und internationale Politik*, 8 (1999), pp. 984–90, here p. 985.

32   Ibid., p. 987. Beck's variation on Clausewitz – 'the continuation of morality by other means' – is evidently directed against Clausewitz's own theory of war, whose validity Beck limits to what he calls the *first modernity*: that is, the epoch in which the principle 'international right overrides human right' applied. In the *second modernity*, with its agenda of postnational wars, the basic principle is rather 'human right overrides international right'. 'This kind of war is postnational because it is not fought

in the national interest (the continuation of politics by other means), and because it cannot be understood in terms of old rivalries among national states in varying degrees hostile to one another' (ibid., p. 984).

33 The following considerations conform in large parts to the model that Philipp Genschel and Klaus Schlichte have developed for the ideo-typical course of civil wars: see Philipp Genschel and Klaus Schlichte, 'Wenn Kriege chronisch werden: Der Bürgerkrieg', *Leviathan*, 25, 4 (1997), pp. 501–17. See also Heinrich-W. Krumwiede and Peter Waldmann, eds, *Civil War: Consequences and Possibilities for Regulation* (Baden-Baden: Nomos Verlag, 2000), and François Jean and Jean-Christophe Rufin, eds, *Économie des guerres civiles* (Paris: Hachette, 1996).

34 See chapter 4, pp. 77ff.

35 See, among others, Wolfgang Kersting, 'Lassen sich Menschenrechte mit Gewalt zwischenstaatlich durchsetzen?', and Véronique Zanetti, 'Menschenrechte und humanitäre Interventionspflicht', both in Gustav Gustenau, ed., *Humanitäre militärische Intervention zwischen Legalität und Legitimität* (Baden-Baden: Nomos Verlag, 2000), pp. 59–92 and 93–107.

36 See chapter 2, pp. 34–41.

37 Ahmed Rashid has powerfully shown that the collapse of the Afghan state, together with the aid given by the Taliban and al-Qaeda to associated rebel movements, had a dramatically destabilizing impact on the republics of Central Asia. See his *Jihad: The Rise of Militant Islam in Central Asia* (New York: Yale University Press, 2002), pp. 209ff.

38 Chomsky's bitter critique of US foreign policy and its much-touted concept of 'rogue states' rests not least upon repeated observation of these double standards. See especially *Rogue States*, pp. 29ff.

39 See Armin A. Steinkamm, 'Völkerrecht, humanitäre Intervention und Legitimation des Bundeswehr-Einsatzes', in Gustenau, *Humanitäre militärische Intervention*, pp. 109–39; and Hajo Schmidt, 'Humanitäre Intervention nach dem Kosovo-Krieg von 1999: Rechtsethische Reflexionen', in Voigt, *Krieg*, pp. 109–30.

40 See John R. MacArthur, *Second Front: Censorship and Propaganda in the Gulf War* (New York: Hill & Wang, 1992); and Mira Beham, *Kriegstrommeln: Medien, Krieg und Politik* (Munich: Deutscher Taschenbuch, 1996).

41 It has often been noted that US society greatly differs in this respect from West European societies; Michael Howard, for instance, writes: 'A Jacksonian bellicosity remains very much part of American popular culture.' But he immediately adds: 'But with it goes the reluctance common to all Western urbanized societies to suffer heavy losses, either civilian or military' (*The Invention of Peace: Reflections on War and International Order* (London: Profile, 2000), p. 102).

42 See Anne Nivat, *Chienne de guerre: A Woman Reporter behind the Lines of the War in Chechnya* (New York: Public Affairs, 2001).

43 The picture has been rather different in Germany, where there was a debate after unification about German involvement in such interventions,

and the Bundeswehr has subsequently been deployed abroad on several occasions. Of course, this is mainly due to the specificities of Germany.

44 See chapter 4, pp. 74ff.

45 See Ignatieff, *Virtual War*, esp. pp. 161ff.

46 This concept may be found in Jürgen Osterhammel, 'Kulturelle Grenzen in der Expansion Europas', *Saeculum*, 46 (1995), pp. 101–38, here pp. 109ff.

47 For a more detailed discussion, see Herfried Münkler, *Der neue Golfkrieg* (Reinbek/Hamburg: Rowohlt, 2003).

INDEX